INTERNAL LABOR MARKETS AND EMPLOYMENT TRANSITIONS IN SOUTH KOREA

Kim Sunghoon

University Press of America,® Inc.
Lanham · Boulder · New York · Toronto · Oxford

University Press of America,® Inc.
4501 Forbes Boulevard
Suite 200
Lanham, Maryland 20706
UPA Acquisitions Department (301) 459-3366

PO Box 317
Oxford
OX2 9RU, UK

Library of Congress Control Number: 2004114176
ISBN 0-7618-3075-8 (clothbound : alk. ppr.)
ISBN 0-7618-3076-6 (paperback : alk. ppr.)

™ The paper used in this publication meets the minimum
requirements of American National Standard for Information
Sciences—Permanence of Paper for Printed Library Materials,
ANSI Z39.48—1984

Contents

List of Figures

List of Tables

Preface

Broadly speaking, my primary sociological interest has been investigating social inequalities. To study social inequalities, I have focused on inequalities in the Korean labor market. This project is the result of my study on labor market inequalities for the last several years. It is my Ph.D. dissertation, with a few revisions.

I owe the completion of this book to many people. First of all, I would like to express my greatest thanks to the chair of my dissertation committee, Professor David Lindstrom. He offered valuable advice at every stage of the dissertation. In particular, his advice on the theoretical framework and the appropriate methods of analysis was invaluable. I am also deeply grateful to my other committee members, Professors Dennis Hogan and Mary Fennell, for their valuable advice on the significance and implications of the study and on many detailed arguments of the dissertation.

I cannot forget to thank the readers, Professors Jose Itzigsohn and Susan Short, for their valuable comments during the dissertation defense. I would like to express my heartfelt thanks to Jennifer Park for proofreading my dissertation in spite of her own demanding work.

I was fortunate to be able to use data from the "East Asia Social Survey on People's Work Life: South Korea," for my project. I would like to thank Professor Song Ho-Keun for introducing me to these excellent data, and Professors Yee Jaeyeol, Kim Yonghak, and Mary Brinton for granting me access to the data and providing me with very useful documents related to the data.

My best friend, colleague, and wife, Woo Myungsook, deserves my special thanks. Without her support and encouragement, it would have been much more difficult for me to complete this project. My family has always been supportive of my work. I especially thank my sister-in-law, Hyunjoo, for not sparing any effort in collecting valuable data for the project. I hope that this book will someday have meaning for my beautiful baby, Hajin.

Kim Sunghoon
Seoul, South Korea
September 2004

1 Introduction

Sociological Questions

Social mobility has been a major topic of sociological research. One of the most important forms of social mobility that has been studied is labor mobility: workers' movements between jobs, workplaces, occupations, industries, or regions. Labor mobility affects workers' economic and social well-being significantly because it usually accompanies considerable changes in their working conditions and social environments. Furthermore, workers' life chances, life styles, and subjective well-being are more influenced by long paths of socioeconomic rewards associated with long-term patterns of labor mobility than by socioeconomic rewards at a particular point in time (Sørensen 2001).

If an employee leaves his or her workplace, the possibility exists that he or she may become (1) a new employee at another workplace, (2) an entrepreneur hiring at least several employees, (3) a self-employed person hiring only a few employees or none, (4) an unemployed person looking for work, (5) or a person out of the labor force. An employee's leaving his or her workplace, called an employment transition in this study, has an especially significant influence on his or her economic and social well-being, for it usually entails conspicuous changes in earnings and working conditions, loss of earnings, or disturbances in various kinds of other life conditions. The explanation of employment transitions is what this study seeks to address.

Two aspects of employment transitions that bear on workers' economic and social well-being are employment stability and the desirability of transition outcomes. In this project, I will answer two sociological questions that are related to these two aspects of employment transitions. The first sociological question is about the way in which the value that employers and workers place on stable employment is modified by individual conditions or resources and by structural factors. The second sociological question is about the way in which the value that workers place on more desirable transition outcomes is modified by individual conditions or resources and by structural factors.

The first aspect of employment transitions related to workers' economic and social well-being—employment stability—is important for both employers and workers. For employers, workers' frequent separations result in a high level of labor management costs and losses of workers' firm-specific skills, knowledge, and experiences that increase labor productivity and profits. For workers, unstable employment usually leads to unstable and unpredictable life conditions that decrease overall quality of life.

The importance of employment stability is stressed by the Japanese "lifetime employment" or "permanent employment" model, which constitutes, along with seniority wages and company unions, a part of "Japanese labor relations (Jung 1992: 5)." In Japanese lifetime employment, large firms "employ only people who have just graduated from school" and "they never fire or lay off employees," and "employees tend to work for their first employer until retirement (Yamaguchi 1992: 285)." In this situation, employees are said to show lifetime commitment and loyalty to firms which lead to increased labor productivity. There have been some criticisms of the Japanese lifetime employment model. Marsh and Mannari (1971) maintain that workers' abilities and skills are more important than seniority in determining wage levels in Japan. Odaka claims that the Japanese lifetime employment system causes such problems as the oppression of employees' creativity and individuality, the emergence of the sector of disadvantaged workers, and the occurrence of labor alienation (Jung 1992: 6). Despite these criticisms, the importance of stable employment for both employers and employees is well-captured by the Japanese lifetime employment model. It is important, therefore, to study individual and structural factors that influence stable employment. The first sociological question above addresses this issue, i.e., exploring factors that influence whether or not a worker leaves his or her workplace.

The second aspect of employment transitions related to workers' economic and social well-being—the desirability of transition outcomes—is important for workers who leave their workplaces. Although workers generally prefer stable employment to unstable employment, they leave their workplaces voluntarily in order to increase their economic and social well-being, or involuntarily under various kinds of circumstances that they cannot avoid. When workers leave their workplaces, an important factor is the economic and social desirability of new destinations. It is important, therefore, to investigate individual and structural factors that cause desirable transition outcomes. The second sociological question addresses this issue, i.e., exploring factors that affect whether or not a worker who has left his or her workplace arrives at a better destination.

It needs to be noted that these two aspects of employment transitions are closely related to each other and constitute a two-stage process experienced by a worker voluntarily or involuntarily. In the first stage, whether a worker leaves his or her workplace influences his or her economic and social well-being. In the second stage, the destination at which a worker arrives after he or she leaves his or her workplace also influences his or her economic and social well-being.

These two stages are closely related to each other in that the second stage is conditional on the first stage.

I will try to answer these sociological questions, which are related to the two aspects of employment transitions, in the context of South Korea (hereafter Korea)—a country that has experienced rapid economic development for the last four decades.

We may presume that some factors influence the two aspects of employment transitions in both Korea and Western countries. One of the most reasonable grounds for this argument is that Korea has achieved a considerable degree of industrialization as found in Western countries. In order to study factors that can be considered to be influential in both Korea and Western countries, I will do the following. First, I will expand on relevant theories and research that have been developed and performed in the context of Western countries. Second, I will examine whether or not these theories have explanatory power in the context of Korea.

We may also presume that some other factors affect the two aspects of employment transitions only in Korea. One of the reasons for this argument may be that Korea industrialized much more rapidly than Western countries. In order to study factors that can be considered to be unique to Korea, I will try to develop theories reflecting Korea's experience of rapid industrialization, and investigate whether or not these theories are supported by results of the analysis.

Trends of Employment Transitions in Korea

In order to show the overall trends of employment transitions and some of the most important factors affecting employment transitions in Korea, I present two kinds of statistics. The first set of statistics shows employment stability over time, and the second shows the composition of working people by employment status over time.

The separation rate is an indicator of employment stability.[1] Figures 1-1, 1-2, and 1-3 show separation rates by industry, gender, and firm size in Korea, respectively.

In Figure 1-1, separation rates in the manufacturing industry need to be looked at more closely because overall, (1) they have been significantly higher than separation rates in the nonmanufacturing industries, (2) they have been influencing separation rates of all industries more strongly than separation rates in the nonmanufacturing industries have, and (3) they began to decrease conspicuously as of the late 1980s compared to separation rates in the nonmanufacturing industries.

Figure 1-2 shows that although the patterns of changes in separation rates for both male and female workers have been similar to those in the manufacturing industry, separation rates have been consistently higher for female workers.

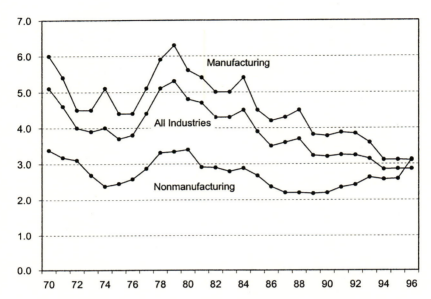

Figure 1-1. Annual Average Monthly Separation Rate in Nonagricultural
          Private Sector: Korea, 1970-1996 (%)
Sources: Ministry of Labor. various years. *Report on Monthly Labor Survey.*

Figure 1-3 shows that among male blue-collar workers in the manufacturing industry, separation rates for workers in larger firms have been lower, and began to decrease conspicuously as of the late 1980s. This implies that since the late 1980s, overall employment stability has been increasing in large firms in Korea.

The statistics presented in Figures 1-1, 1-2, and 1-3 imply that differences in industry, gender, and firm size, and their changes over time need to be considered when employment stability in Korea is investigated.

As a result of Korea's rapid industrialization during the last four decades, there has been a dramatic decrease in the size of rural population, most of which has consisted of self-employed farmers. The rapid industrialization has also led to a dramatic increase in the number of urban employees. One of the peculiar results of Korea's industrialization has been a persistence of a significant proportion of urban self-employed people (Kim et al. 1999: 50).

As seen in Figure 1-4, in 1963, the employed comprised 31.5 percent of the entire working population, and the self-employed comprised 37.2 percent. In 1996, the proportion of the employed was 62.8 percent, and that of the self-employed was 27.9 percent. Considering that the proportion of those working in

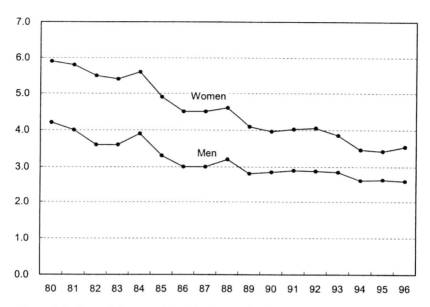

Figure 1-2. Annual Average Monthly Separation Rate in Nonagricultural
Private Sector by Gender: Korea, 1980-1996 (%)
Sources: Ministry of Labor. various years. *Report on Monthly Labor Survey.*

the primary industry (including agriculture, forestry, and fishery) decreased
from 63.0 percent to 11.6 percent between 1963 and 1996 (Figure 1-5), one
notices that the major proportion of the self-employed changed from self-
employed farmers to urban self-employed people.

These dramatic changes in the proportion of employees and in the characteristics of the self-employed must have had significant influences on the entire
working population's earnings, job opportunities, and employment stability. If
we only look at changes in the composition of the working population by
employment status over time, however, we cannot understand the importance of
changes in the proportion of each group properly. For example, if movements
between self-employment and other employment statuses have been frequent, a
significant part of the labor force has been self-employed during their work
careers even though the proportion of the self-employed has decreased (Kim et
al. 1999: 62). Therefore, it is necessary to explore the *rates* of changes in employment status over time. Studying factors that affect these rates will enable
one to understand the mechanisms through which changes in employment status
occur.

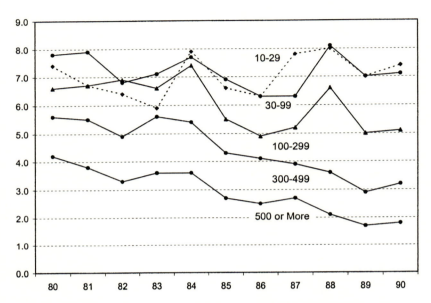

Figure 1-3. Annual Average Monthly Separation Rate of Male Blue-Collar
Workers in Manufacturing Industry by Firm Size (Number of
Employees): Korea, 1980-1990 (%)
Sources: Ministry of Labor. various years. *Report on Monthly Labor Survey.*

Outline of the Study

Factors affecting the rates of employment transitions consist of various individual and structural factors, changes in those factors over time, and interactions
between those factors. This study will focus on labor market structure, its
changes over time, and its interactions with other individual and structural
factors. There are four reasons for choosing labor market structure as the key
factor in this study.

First, I expect that labor market structure plays a crucial role in shaping long-
term patterns of employment transitions. In fact, some types of labor market
structures—such as internal labor market structure, which will be discussed in
detail later in this study—are devised for the purpose of playing such a role
(Sørensen 2001). We need to examine whether these structures actually fulfill
their intended goal.

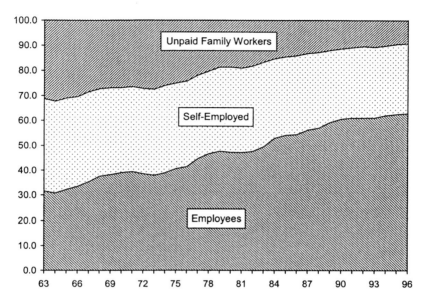

Figure 1-4. Composition of Working Population by Employment Status:
Korea, 1963-1996 (%)
Source: National Statistical Office (1998).

Second, labor market structure can interact with other factors in influencing the rates of employment transitions. By investigating these interactions, I will make clear the effects of labor market structure on differences in employment stability and in the desirability of transition outcomes among various types of Korean workers.

Third, as mentioned above, the proportion of urban employees has dramatically increased as a result of the rapid economic development in Korea since the early 1960s. This means that the relationship between labor supply and labor demand has fundamentally changed in the Korean labor market. Before Korea began to industrialize rapidly, most Koreans worked in the agricultural sector. As industrialization continued, unskilled workers were freely supplied to the industrial sector. At this time, wages were determined at the level of subsistence according to classical economics. As industrialization proceeded further, this unlimited supply of unskilled labor ended. According to neoclassical economists, wages were now determined by marginal labor productivity (Lewis 1954). Bai

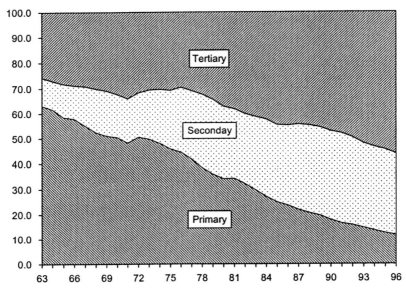

Figure 1-5. Composition of Working Population by Industry: Korea, 1963-
     1996 (%)
Source: National Statistical Office (1998).

(1989: 108) claims that unlimited supply of unskilled labor from the agricultural
to the industrial sectors ended around 1975 in Korea. By acknowledging the
basic importance of the labor market for working people's economic activities
and earnings, one also acknowledges the importance of labor market structure
and its changes over time in understanding the mechanisms by which employment transitions occur.

   Fourth, despite such importance, the labor market structure in Korea has
rarely been considered in research on various kinds of labor mobility or employment transitions. One of the main contributions of this project is to fill this
research gap.

   The following describes the project's plan in detail. First, I will show that
different types of labor market structures have differently affected Korean
workers' rates of employment transitions.

   Second, in addition to type of labor market structure, I will include other important individual and structural variables in the analysis. Since previous research has shown that individual-level factors such as human capital have a
significant influence on employment transition rates, I will also include human

capital in the analysis. Important organization-level characteristics, such as whether an organization is large and whether it is unionized—characteristics that have rarely been addressed—will be included in the analysis, too. Gender will be added in the analysis to explore whether or not Korean women, who have suffered from various kinds of economic and social disadvantages in the labor market, show different patterns of employment transitions than Korean men. Whereas most previous research has analyzed employment transition rates separately by gender, I will analyze data containing both men and women in order to investigate whether gender influences the rates of employment transitions in Korea. By using a set of dummy variables that reflect both gender and gender-related factors such as childcare and housework, I will investigate whether these gender-related factors influence the rates of employment transitions in Korea. I will further explore whether or not labor market structure interacts with each of these individual and structural variables to test for differences in the effects of these variables on employment transition rates by type of labor market structure.

Third, I will add chronological time, i.e., calendar year, as a proxy for macro-level factors in order to investigate the influences of changes in the structure of the economy and in the state's labor market policies on employment transition rates. Furthermore, by analyzing an interaction between labor market structure and calendar year, I will test for changes in the effects of labor market structure on employment transition rates over time. These changes over time will be interpreted in terms of important turning points in the structure of the economy and in the state's labor market policies in Korea.

Fourth, cohort size effects may be important. Korea has experienced significant population growth and, accordingly, a significant growth of the working-age population during the last four decades. Cohort size effects, therefore, will also be included in the analysis.

In the next chapter, I will explain the process of economic development and the changes in the labor market in Korea from 1953 through 1996 in order to show the context of employment transition patterns in Korea. In Chapter 3, I will specify theoretical models that are relevant to the study by reviewing and expanding previous sociological research on the subject. In Chapter 4, appropriate data and methods for the study will be shown. Since the study of factors affecting employment stability can best be performed using event history methods and event history data, I will show how to use event history methods and how to construct appropriate event history data. I will also explain how to operationalize the dependent and independent variables of the analysis in Chapter 4. Chapters 5 and 6 will be devoted to specifying detailed working hypotheses and presenting and discussing results of the analysis. In Chapter 7, I will summarize results of the analysis, discuss the implications of the results for two sociological questions posed earlier in this chapter, address the limitations of the study, and propose a future research agenda.

Notes

1 The separation rate is calculated as follows.

Separation Rate = {(number of employees separating from employers for a current month) / (number of employees at the end of the previous month)} × 100.

2 Economic Development and Employment Transitions in Korea

The economic structure and the state's labor market policies have significantly influenced patterns of employment transitions through their considerable effects on labor market conditions and labor relations in Korea. Therefore, investigating changes in patterns of employment transitions requires examination of changes in Korea's economic structure, labor market policies, and their influence on labor market conditions and labor relations.

In this chapter, the Korean economic development from 1953 to 1996 will be described focusing on changes in the structure of the Korean economy, labor market policies, and their influences on changes in labor market conditions and labor relations. I will explain changes in the economic structure in terms of changes in the state's economic development strategies. On the basis of these investigations, I will present expectations about the influences of changes in the structure of the Korean economy and in the state's labor market policies on employment transition patterns over time.

Due to the low degree of capital accumulation in the private sector during the 1950s, the Korean state assumed the role of promoting economic development since the early 1960s. In order to conceptualize the main characteristics of the Korean state's strategies of economic development, I use the concept of export-oriented industrialization (EOI) (Gereffi 1990: 17). EOI is an outward-looking strategy of economic development and involves the efforts of achieving industrialization by producing the goods that are to be exported. There are primary and secondary phases for EOI. In the primary phase, labor-intensive manufactures are the main products. In the secondary phase, which is a more advanced phase than the primary phase, capital- and technology-intensive manufactures are the main products. These two subtypes of development strategies—primary EOI and secondary EOI—correspond to several stages of the rapid economic development in Korea, and are related to some of the most important political events and environments since the end of the Korean War.[1]

1953-1960: Underdeveloped Economy

Korea's underdeveloped economy in the 1950s was foreshadowed by the political, social, and economic unrest caused by the division of the Korean peninsula into South and North Koreas in 1945, ending 35 years of Japanese colonialism. It is estimated that production in 1948 was only 20 percent of production in 1940 (Kim 1992: 68). The Korean War from 1950 to 1953 left the Korean economy even more devastated. Gross national product (GNP) per capita dropped from $67 in 1949 to $55 in 1953 (Kim 1992: 67).

Any systematic and coordinated development strategies of the state were not possible due to wide-spread political corruption of President Rhee's regime. The United States played a major role in maintaining Korea's sluggish economy by providing economic aid. The average annual inflow of U.S. aid from 1953 through 1958 was about 15 percent of the average annual GNP and over 80 percent of foreign exchange (Amsden 1992: 39). U.S. aid, however, was not very helpful to Korea's industrialization. Of the total aid-financed imports, only 3.4 percent in 1953 and 11.7 percent in 1960 were capital goods such as machinery and transportation equipment, so that little foreign aid was invested in production facilities (Amsden 1992: 45).

Moreover, the Rhee regime provided favored entrepreneurs with U.S. aid in the form of loans at subsidized interest rates in exchange for political campaign contributions. Favored entrepreneurs who were given subsidized loans operated in a wide range of industries although textile was the most important industry (Amsden 1992: 38-9). The fact that favored entrepreneurs invested subsidized loans in a wide range of industries meant that Korea was in the phase of import-substitution industrialization, but it also meant that Korea lacked any systematic development strategies. Consequently, economic growth was slow, and the industrial sector was much less important than the nonindustrial sectors in the Korean economy throughout the 1950s.[2]

As a result of the underdeveloped economy and slow economic growth, Korean workers generally experienced poor material conditions. The proportion of workers in the industrial sector was low.[3] New employment opportunities in the labor market were rare. The unemployment rate was estimated at 20 percent in 1960 (Amsden 1992: 48), and the ratio of job offers to job seekers was 0.70 in 1960 (Bai 1991: 275). Workers in the industrial sector earned low wages.[4] Poor working conditions prevailed in the aftermath of wartime economy in which firm organizations and job specifications had been little developed (Song 1991: 113). Working hours were very long on average because Korea's factory system originated in the harsh colonial factory system that had been characterized by a long workweek (Amsden 1992: 206).

One of the main reasons why workers in the industrial sector suffered from low wages and poor working conditions was that excessive population in the agricultural sector and the urban informal sector put pressure on wage rates of workers in the industrial sector. Although various political and economic rights for workers were articulated in the Constitution and labor laws, which imitated the constitutions and labor laws of the then-advanced capitalist countries, most of them were not enforced strictly (Kim 1982: 195-6). Even if workers did not receive wages on time, had to do additional work without extra wages, or did not receive any compensations for injuries at the workplace, the government generally did not enforce labor laws to protect workers.

From both aspects of union density and ideological inclination, labor movements were too weak to significantly improve workers' political rights and material conditions. The numbers of labor unions and union members were small and did not increase much before 1960 when student-led demonstrations overthrew the Rhee regime.[5] Radical labor movements had already been crushed by the American occupation forces and the newly-born Korean government by 1949. The ensuing Korean War consolidated the domination of conservative anti-communist labor movements (Bai 1989: 352-3). The General Federation of Korean Trade Unions was virtually a subsidiary agency of the ruling Liberal Party. Its main object was to serve the political interests of the Rhee regime, not to improve workers' political rights and material conditions (Bai 1989: 354-5).

In short, slow industrialization left the industrial sector insignificant, and workers in industrial labor markets suffered from low wages and poor working conditions in Korea in the 1950s.

1961-1971: Primary EOI

Major General Park Chung-Hee took power through a coup d'état in 1961. In order to legitimize the coup, he proclaimed that the main goals of the junta were reinforcement of anti-communism, eradication of corruption, and elimination of poverty through economic development. Of these goals, elimination of poverty through economic development required the most systematic and consistent efforts of the state. The establishment of the Economic Planning Board (EPB) in 1961 was one of the first steps of such efforts. The main missions of the EPB were to formulate comprehensive and long-term plans for the development of the national economy and to implement them (Kim 1997: 102).

The state maintained that the only way for Korea to achieve rapid economic growth was to pursue the strategy of primary EOI. The state, however, did not intend to assume the role of the most important producer. The state conferred largely the role of the most important producer to private firms by providing them with "performance-based incentives (Amsden 1992: 14)." The state gave favored firms preferential financing, preferential tariffs, and tax breaks. In return, favored firms had to show good performance in exporting their products. If they failed to show good performance, the state generally stopped providing them with the above benefits and did not save them from bankruptcy. Successful firms grew to be business conglomerates and assumed the role of the key producer in the Korean economy. In this period, their main products were labor-intensive because the international competitiveness of the Korean economy was mainly based on low wages in labor-intensive industries. EOI in the 1960s, therefore, was primary EOI.

As illustrated in Figure 1-5 in the previous chapter, the rapid industrialization through primary EOI rapidly increased the number of workers in the nonagricultural sectors. Consequently, employment opportunities in the labor market increased rapidly, too. The unemployment rate dropped from 8.1 percent in 1963 to 4.4 percent in 1971, and the ratio of job offers to job seekers, which was 0.70 in 1960, rose to 0.92 in 1971 (Table 2-1).

As GNP grew quickly during the mid-1960s, real wages also increased fairly quickly beginning in the late 1960s (Table 2-1). However, the wage level for workers in the industrial sector was still low.[6] In fact, the rate of increase in real wages was lower than the rate of increase in labor productivity in 1971 (Table 2-1). Working conditions did not improve much either. For example, the length of working hours for Korean workers was exceptionally long (Amsden 1992: 206): The annual average weekly working hours was 50.6 hours in 1971 (Table 2-1).

Some of the important factors that contributed to low wages in the 1960s were a low wage base, the state's cheap labor policy, and the plentiful labor supply from the agricultural sector. First, the fact that the industrial sector was small and underdeveloped in the 1950s meant that Korea's primary EOI started from a very low wage base (Amsden 1992: 202). Therefore, the wage level was still low throughout the 1960s even though primary EOI led to rapid economic growth in the same period.

Second, the state tried to keep the Korean economy's international competitiveness of low wages through its cheap labor policy. On the one hand, the state enforced the wage increase rate not to exceed the sum of the rate of increase in the consumer price index and the rate of increase in the labor productivity index (Shin 1994: 200). On the other hand, the state did little to raise the wages of the workers who earned the lowest wages (Yee 1983: 226). Furthermore, the state began to aggressively intervene in labor relations to suppress workers' collective demands for wage increases and improvements in working conditions (Bai 1989: 307-8). The Labor Bureau was reorganized and raised to the Labor Office in 1963 to enforce labor policies more actively. Workers in firms established by foreign capital were prohibited by a provisional special law in 1970 from establishing labor unions. As a result, the average union density in 1963-1971 was only 11.8 percent (Table 2-1). Although the state revised labor laws to improve workers' economic welfare to some extent as the Korean economy grew rapidly, its repressive labor policies characterized this period of primary EOI.

Third, as shown in Figure 1-5 in the previous chapter, the proportion of the labor force in the agricultural sector remained fairly high throughout the 1960s, although it decreased substantially. As a result, the agricultural sector still supplied the nonagricultural sectors with large additional labor force, and the plentiful labor supply from the agricultural sector checked wage increases in the

Table 2-1. Indices of Economic Development and Labor Market: Korea, 1961-1971

Year	(A) Unemployment Rate (%)	(B) Ratio of Job Offers to Job Seekers	(C) GNP/capita in Current Prices ($)	(D) GNP Growth Rate* (%)	(E) Real Wage Index	(F) Real Wage Increase Rate (%)	(G) Labor Productivity Index	(H) Labor Productivity Increase Rate (%)	(I) Weekly Working Hours	(J) Union Density (%)
1961			82	5.6						
1962			87	2.2						
1963	8.1		100	9.1	100.0	1.3				9.4
1964	7.7		103	9.6						11.5
1965	7.3		105	5.8						11.6
1966	7.1		125	12.7	101.9	0.6				11.8
1967	6.1		142	6.6	112.1	10.0				12.4
1968	5.0	0.91	169	11.3						12.1
1969	4.7	0.93	210	13.8	141.3	13.0				12.5
1970	4.4	0.94	253	7.6	150.2	6.2	100.0		51.6	12.6
1971	4.4	0.92	289	8.0	158.1	5.2	108.8	8.8	50.6	12.7
Mean	6.1	0.92		8.4						11.8

Sources: A, B, C, D, I – NSO (1998); E, F – Amsden (1992: 197); G, H – Cho (1992: 294); J – Kim (1991: 209).
Definitions:
    E = nominal wage index / consumer price index × 100.
    G = index for (total output / number of workers in production).
    J = number of union members / number of total employees × 100.
Subjects:
    E, F: Mining and manufacturing workers.
    G, H: Blue-collar workers in mining, manufacturing, electricity, gas, and waterworks.
    I: Workers in nonagricultural firms employing 10 or more workers.
* Calculated from data in constant 1990 prices in the Korean currency.

nonagricultural sectors as it had usually done in the early stages of industrialization in other countries.

1972-1986: Secondary EOI

The Park regime replaced the existing constitution with the Revitalizing Reforms Constitution through a popular referendum in October 1972. The Revitalizing Reforms Constitution changed the political system of Korea dramatically by changing the direct presidential election system to an indirect system, weakening the power of the national assembly, and concentrating enormous power in the presidency. This political move was the regime's response to a growing arms race against North Korea and increasing social, political, and economic problems and tensions that rapid economic growth in the 1960s had created. Although this harsh dictatorship ended with the assassination of President Park in 1979, the succeeding president, Chun Doo Hwan, who had been a military general and had also taken power through a coup, maintained severe authoritarianism until 1987.

The development strategies in this period were mainly characterized by secondary EOI, which is a more advanced phase than primary EOI. More specifically, secondary EOI meant heavy-industrialization. The state strongly encouraged business conglomerates to initiate heavy industries such as shipbuilding, steel, automobile, and petrochemical industries. One of the principal goals of Korean heavy-industrialization was to gain an advantage over North Korea in the arms race, for heavy-industrialization usually enables a country to build a munitions industry more easily. Another principal goal of Korean heavy-industrialization was to substitute domestic high value-added industrial products for imports. To deepen the structure of the Korean economy in order to survive international economic competitions was another important goal. The state maintained that the Korean economy had to be transformed into an economy that could produce and export higher value-added industrial products in order to survive international competitions. Heavy-industrialization made such transformation of the economy possible because the main manufactures of heavy industries, which were capital- and technology-intensive, were generally higher value-added.

The state tried to achieve these goals by granting business conglomerates various kinds of benefits such as cheap loans and reduced taxes. These benefits were crucial in enticing business conglomerates into building the munitions industry and producing domestically and exporting high value-added industrial products that had been imported. The principle of providing "performance-based incentives" was still in effect in this period. As in the phase of primary EOI, business conglomerates had to show good performance in export in order to continue to receive the above benefits from the state.

The rapid industrialization through secondary EOI continued to increase the proportion of workers in the nonagricultural sectors rapidly as shown in Figure 1-5 in the previous chapter. As a result, employment opportunities in the labor market continued to increase. The unemployment rates were largely lower in 1972-1986 than they had been in 1963-1971, and the ratios of job offers to job seekers were largely higher in 1972-1986 than they had been in 1963-1971 (Tables 2-1 and 2-2).

As GNP continued to grow rapidly in 1972-1986, so did real wages (Table 2-2). The rates of increases in real wages, however, were still lower than the rates of increases in labor productivity in this period (Table 2-2). Working conditions remained poor. For example, average working hours was among the longest in the world (Amsden 1992: 205; Table 2-2).

One of the main reasons why increases in wages were not proportional to workers' contributions to the rapid economic growth in Korea was that the state continued to enforce its cheap labor policy. The state set official guidelines for the annual wage increase rates. Although the actual wage increase rates exceeded the state's guidelines in 1972-1979 due to high inflation caused by the heavy-industrialization of secondary EOI, they were generally kept under the state's guidelines in 1980-1986 when the state succeeded in checking inflation (Table 2-3; Song 1991: 275-85).

The state's wage guideline policy was backed up by the state's intensified intervention in the labor market and labor relations (Bai 1989: 308-9). Labor laws were revised in the early 1970s to suppress workers' collective actions more easily although the revised labor laws aimed to improve workers' economic welfare to some extent. The rights to collective bargaining and action could now be restricted by presidential decrees. The Revitalizing Reforms Constitution stipulated that workers' basic rights were to be restricted by relevant lower-level labor laws. The authority to judge whether or not a labor dispute is legal was transferred from the Labor Commission, which consisted of 3 representatives of labor, 3 representatives of management, and 3-5 representatives of the public interest, to the Labor Office.

The restrictions on workers' collective actions became more severe in the early 1980s although labor laws were revised to improve workers' economic welfare to some degree, and the restrictions in the Revitalizing Reforms Constitution on workers' basic rights were removed in the new constitution. The Labor Office was raised to the Ministry of Labor in 1981 to better manage the capital's increased need for state intervention in the labor market and labor relations. The industrial union system was changed to an enterprise union system. Third parties (other than an employer and an enterprise union) were prohibited from involvement in a labor dispute. All these measures made workers' collective actions very difficult and weakened workers' bargaining power as reflected in declining union density in the early 1980s (Table 2-3). The state's repressive labor policies, however, increased workers' dissatisfaction with the authoritarian regime as well. Workers' increasing dissatisfaction was one of the main factors that made possible the partial political democratization in 1987.

One of the most important changes in the labor market in this period was that workers in large firms, which were created as a result of heavy-industrialization, began to enjoy some advantages in terms of wages and working conditions over

Table 2-2. Indices of Economic Development and Labor Market: Korea, 1972-
1986

Year	(A) Unemployment Rate (%)	(B) Ratio of Job Offers to Job Seekers	(C) GNP/ capita in Current Prices ($)	(D) GNP Growth Rate* (%)	(E) Real Wage Index	(F) Real Wage Increase Rate (%)	(G) Labor Productivity Index	(H) Labor Productivity Increase Rate (%)	(I) Weekly Working Hours	(J) Union Density (%)
1972	4.5	0.93	319	4.6	100.0	5.0	100.0	7.7	50.9	12.9
1973	3.9	1.03	396	12.6	107.8	7.8	108.4	8.4	50.7	13.2
1974	4.0	0.88	541	8.0	113.6	5.4	119.4	10.2	49.6	14.8
1975	4.1	0.95	594	6.1	118.0	3.9	132.4	10.9	50.0	15.8
1976	3.9	0.92	802	11.9	138.7	17.5	141.5	6.8	50.7	16.5
1977	3.8	1.05	1,011	10.1	166.5	20.0	155.9	10.2	51.4	16.7
1978	3.2	1.16	1,400	9.4	195.9	17.7	173.8	11.5	51.3	16.9
1979	3.8	1.23	1,647	6.8	212.2	8.3	200.7	15.5	50.5	16.8
1980	5.2	1.02	1,597	-3.9	203.5	-4.1	221.5	10.4	51.6	14.7
1981	4.5	0.99	1,741	5.5	202.4	-0.5	258.2	16.6	51.9	14.6
1982	4.4	0.89	1,834	7.5	218.8	8.1	274.7	6.4	52.1	14.4
1983	4.1	1.20	2,014	12.2	234.9	7.4	310.4	13.0	52.5	14.1
1984	3.8	1.05	2,187	8.5	249.9	6.4	337.2	8.6	52.4	13.2
1985	4.0	0.97	2,242	6.6	266.8	6.8	352.7	4.6	51.9	12.4
1986	3.8	1.02	2,568	11.9	280.8	5.3	411.3	16.6	52.5	12.3
Mean	4.1	1.02		7.9		7.7		10.5	51.3	14.6

Sources: A, B, C, E, F, I – NSO (1998); G, H – Cho (1992: 294); J – Kim (1991: 209).
Definitions: Same as in Table 2-1.
Subjects:
   E, F: Nonagricultural workers.
   G, H (1972-1979): Blue-collar workers in mining, manufacturing, electricity, gas, and
                waterworks.
   G, H (1980-1986): Regular workers in mining, manufacturing, electricity, gas, and
                waterworks.
   I: Same as in Table 2-1.
* Calculated in the same way as in Table 2-1.

workers in small firms. Another important change in the labor market was that
the plentiful labor supply from the agricultural to the industrial sectors ended
around 1975. As a result, beginning in the late 1970s, the Korean labor market

Table 2-3. Indices of Wage Increases: Korea, 1971-1987

Year	Wage Increase (%)		Wage Drift (A-B)
	Nominal (A)	State's Guideline (B)	
1971	15.4	16.5	-0.9
1972	17.5	14.0	3.5
1973	11.5	9.0	2.5
1974	31.9	25.0	6.9
1975	29.5	26.0	3.5
1976	35.5	16.0	19.5
1977	32.1	18.0	14.1
1978	35.0	19.0	16.0
1979	28.3	15.0	13.3
1980	23.4	28.0	-4.6
1981	20.7	28.0	-7.3
1982	15.8	10.9	4.9
1983	11.0	13.0	-2.0
1984	8.7	10.0	-1.3
1985	9.2	7.3	1.9
1986	8.2	12.1	-3.9
1987	14.3		
1971-1979	26.3	20.1*	8.7
1980-1987	13.9	10.7	-1.8

Source: Song (1991: 269).
B = (inflation rate × 0.7) + (productivity increase rate× 0.8).
* 1971-1981.

tended to become tighter as the unemployment rates and the ratios of job offers to job seekers in Table 2-2 show.

1987-1996: Political Democratization

Growing demands of workers and students for political democratization resulted in partial relaxation of authoritarianism in 1987; this democratization continues today. In 1987, many restrictions on workers' collective actions and on the establishment and activities of labor unions were relaxed, and labor laws were revised to further improve workers' economic welfare and female workers' working conditions (Bai 1989: 311-4). The growing influence of the working class over social and political issues was reflected in the rapid increase in union density in 1988 and 1989 (Table 2-4).[7]

However, the main characteristic of the state's development strategies did not change. The continuing strategy of secondary EOI enabled Korea to deepen its economic structure further and to continue its rapid economic growth. As the proportion of workers in the nonagricultural sectors continued to increase in this period, employment opportunities continued to increase as well. The unemployment rate dropped to 2.0 percent in 1996, and the average ratio of job offers to job seekers, which was 1.02 in 1972-1986, increased to 1.16 in 1987-1996 (Table 2-4).

As GNP continued to increase rapidly in this period, real wages also continued to increase. The rates of increases in real wages, however, were largely still lower than the rates of increases in labor productivity (Table 2-4). As a result of workers' increasing bargaining power and deepening economic structure, workers gained some ground in terms of working conditions. For example, average weekly working hours, which was 51.3 hours in 1972-1986, dropped to 48.6 hours in 1987-1996 (Table 2-4), although it was still among the longest in the world (Lee 1991: 308).

One of the most important ramifications of the industrial deepening in this period was that the state began to experience difficulty in controlling business conglomerates (Kim 1997: 181-203). Growing influences of business conglomerates also meant that the proportion of workers in business conglomerates was growing, and that economic advantages for them were increasing. Political democratization intensified this tendency, for it enabled workers in business conglomerates to pursue their economic interests more easily with their increased bargaining power.

Consequently, economic advantages for workers in large firms over workers in small firms generally increased in this period (Jung 1992: 51-3). The ratios of hourly wages in firms employing 500 workers or more to hourly wages in firms employing 10-99 workers in the manufacturing industry were 1.03 in 1981, 1.06 in 1984, 1.03 in 1987, 1.25 in 1989, and 1.23 in 1990, after controlling for various human capital measures such as years in the labor market, years with the current employer, and education level. The corresponding figures for total wages were 1.15 in 1984, 1.09 in 1987, and 1.26 in 1989. In the meantime, the corresponding figures for monthly working hours were 1.08 in 1984 and 1.02 in 1989.

These results mean that the degree to which workers in large firms earned higher wages than workers in small firms increased in this period even though the degree to which the former worked more hours than the latter decreased. In short, labor market segmentation by firm size intensified in Korea as of around 1987.

Table 2-4. Indices of Economic Development and Labor Market: Korea, 1987-
   1996

Year	(A) Unemployment Rate (%)	(B) Ratio of Job Offers to Job Seekers	(C) GNP/capita in Current Prices ($)	(D) GNP Growth Rate* (%)	(D) Real Wage Index	(E) Real Wage Increase Rate (%)	(F) Labor Productivity Index	(G) Labor Productivity Increase Rate (%)	(H) Weekly Working Hours	(I) Union Density (%)
1987	3.1	1.24	3,218	12.3	100.0	6.8	100.0	11.7	51.9	13.8
1988	2.5	1.28	4,295	12.0	107.8	7.8	111.9	11.9	51.1	17.8
1989	2.6	1.18	5,210	6.9	123.6	14.6	119.7	6.9	49.2	18.7
1990	2.4	1.18	5,883	9.6	135.3	9.5	136.2	13.8	48.2	17.2
1991	2.3	1.21	6,757	9.1	145.4	7.5	155.3	14.0	47.9	15.9
1992	2.4	1.24	6,988	5.0	157.6	8.4	172.2	10.9	47.5	15.0
1993	2.8	1.09	7,484	5.8	168.7	7.0	185.9	8.0	47.5	14.2
1994	2.4	1.11	8,467	8.4	179.0	6.1	205.3	10.4	47.4	13.5
1995	2.0	1.09	10,037	8.7	190.5	6.4	226.6	10.4	47.7	12.7
1996	2.0	0.98	10,543	6.9	203.2	6.7	254.7	12.4	47.3	12.2
Mean	2.5	1.16		8.5		8.1		11.0	48.6	15.1

Sources: A, B, C, E, F, I – NSO (1998); G and H (1987-1990) – Cho (1992: 294); G and
   H (1991-1996) – KLI (1998); J (1987-1989) – Kim (1991: 209); J (1990-1996)
   – KLI (1998).
Definitions: Same as in Table 2-1.
Subjects:
   E, F: Same as in Table 2-2.
   G, H: Regular workers in mining, manufacturing, electricity, gas, and waterworks.
   I: Same as in Table 2-1.
* Calculated in the same way as in Table 2-1.

Effects of Time on Employment Transition Patterns

The effects of time on employment transition patterns consist of diverse aspects.
The discussion in this chapter showed that among such aspects, two aspects
were especially important in the context of Korea: (1) the effects of changes in
the economic structure, i.e., the effects of industrial deepening—which means
the increase in the relative importance of heavy industry to the entire economy—and (2) the effects of changes in the state's labor market policies, i.e., the
effects of partial relaxation of strict state labor controls.

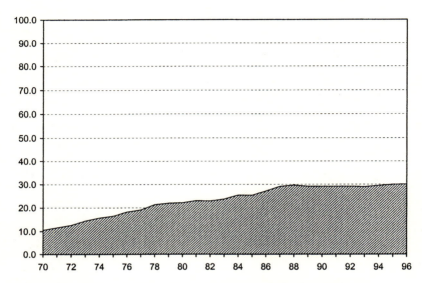

Figure 2-1. Share of Manufacturing in GDP: Korea, 1970-1996 (%)
Sources: Bank of Korea. various years. *National Income Accounts.*

First, the relative importance of heavy industry to the entire economy increased dramatically in Korea during its rapid industrialization, especially
during secondary EOI based on heavy-industrialization. Figure 2-1 shows that
the share of the manufacturing industry in GDP increased from 10.6 percent in
1970 to 30.3 percent in 1997, and Figure 2-2 shows that the share of heavy
industry in the total value-added of the manufacturing industry increased from
38.2 percent in 1965 to 73.4 percent in 1995.

Manufactures of heavy industry are generally capital- and technology-
intensive, so that technologies and work organizations in heavy industry are
more complex than those in light industry. More complex technologies and work
organizations make stable employment more valuable, and enable workers to
accumulate more easily skills, knowledge, and earnings that are helpful in
moving on to better work positions elsewhere. I suggest, therefore, that the rise
in the relative importance of heavy industry in the entire economy increased
workers' employment stability and the likelihood of workers' having better
transition outcomes in Korea.

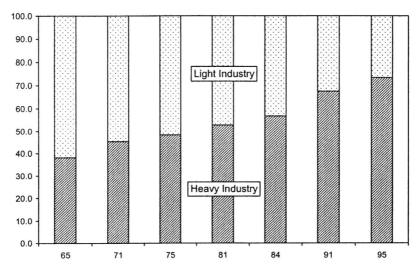

Figure 2-2. Share of Light and Heavy Industries in Total Value-Added of
Manufacturing: Korea, 1965-1995 (%)
Sources: National Statistical Office. various years. *Report on the Survey of the
Mining and Manufacturing Industries.*

Second, one of the most important characteristics of the Korean labor market
during this period of rapid industrialization was that wages were strictly controlled and leveled by the state. This does not mean that the state suppressed
wage levels and kept them very low; rather it means that although significant
wage increases occurred, the rates of increases in wages were generally lower
than the rates of increases in labor productivity and were mainly based on
individual factors such as education, gender, and age, so that wage differentials
based on structural factors such as labor market structure, firm size, and unionism were minimized (Kim et al. 1999: 15-7).

The state tried to minimize the influences of structural factors on wage levels
because strong labor movements could emerge if workers in potentially favorable structural positions could accumulate greater resources. Workers are more
likely to move to other workplaces in order to maximize their wages in the
situation where structural factors are insignificant in determining wage levels
than in the situation where structural factors play a more important role in
determining wage levels. Furthermore, if structural factors are insignificant in
determining wage levels, workers in seemingly favorable structural positions are

not likely to accumulate more earnings that are helpful in moving on to better work positions elsewhere.

The state's strict labor controls, however, were partially relaxed after the onset of political democratization and active labor movements in 1987, which enabled structural factors to play a more important role in determining wage levels. I suggest, therefore, that partial relaxation of strict state labor controls increased employment stability and the likelihood of workers' having better transition outcomes in Korea after 1986.[8]

The expectations presented in this section so far about the influences of changes in the economic structure and in the state's labor market policies on employment transition patterns in Korea can be summarized as follows.

- **Workers showed higher employment stability and more desirable transition outcomes after 1986 than before 1987.**

Notes

1 The following classification of Korea's industrialization periods is based on Song (1995: 36).

2 Korea's real gross domestic product (GDP) grew at about 4 percent annually during the 1950s (Gereffi 1990: 10). In 1960, the industrial sector accounted for only 15.7 percent of GNP, whereas the agricultural sector 36.8 percent, and the service sector 47.5 percent (Kim 1992: 75).

3 In 1960, the industrial sector accounted for only 9 percent of the total labor force, whereas the service sector 25 percent, and the agricultural sector 66 percent (Kim 1992: 93).

4 The following data show that the wage rate for workers in the industrial sector (C) was lower than the wage rate for most workers in the nonindustrial sectors in 1960 (Bai 1991: 272).

Sector	Wage Rate Index
A	135
B	115
C	100
D	70

A = Manufacturing firms hiring 5-9 employees
B = Agriculture, male
C = Textile firms hiring more than 10 employees
D = Agriculture, female

5 The numbers of labor unions were 562 in 1955 and 558 in 1959. The numbers of union members were 205,511 in 1955 and 280,438 in 1959 (Bai 1989: 354).

6 The following data show that the wage rate for workers in the industrial sector (C) was still lower than the wage rate for male workers in the agricultural sector in 1971 (Bai 1991: 272).

Sector	Wage Rate Index
A	81
B	130
C	100
D	90

A = Manufacturing firms hiring 5-9 employees
B = Agriculture, male
C = Textile firms hiring more than 10 employees
D = Agriculture, female

7 Although union density began to decrease again after 1989 due to the counterattack by the state and capital (Table 2-4), labor movements remained more militant and influential in social and political issues since 1987.

8 One might argue that the lifting of wage controls by the state would result in lower employment stability, i.e., higher transition rates, with wage inflation. In order for this to happen, the lifting of wage controls by the state should influence workers across-the-board or mainly workers in less favorable structural positions. In Korea since 1987, however, it has mainly influenced workers in more favorable structural positions, because the main target of the state's strict wage controls was workers in more favorable structural positions until 1986. Consequently, I expect that overall employment stability increased in Korea after 1986, for the transition rates of workers in more favorable structural positions have decreased due to their increased wages.

3 Theories on Employment Transitions

Mechanisms of Employment Transitions

Chapter 1 posed the following sociological question: How is the value that employers and workers place on stable employment modified by individual and structural factors? I make two assumptions to answer this question.

To begin with, I assume that employers and workers try to increase socioeconomic gains, in other words, employers try to increase profits, and workers try to increase wages and improve working conditions. In this study, working conditions consist of various characteristics of workplaces and jobs that are related to workers' economic and social well-being. Working conditions include, for example, length of working hours, physical condition of the workplace, and degree of worker autonomy such as work flexibility, opportunities for creativity, and control over work. Furthermore, I assume that employers want an employment relationship to be continued if they believe that the employment relationship increases profits, and that workers will remain if they believe that the employment relationship increases wages and improves working conditions.

The mechanism through which more stable employment occurs, therefore, is that if employers believe that an individual or structural characteristic increases profits, and/or if workers believe that an individual or structural characteristic increases wages and improves working conditions, that individual or structural characteristic increases employment stability.

I suggest that the most important way in which employers try to increase employment stability is providing workers with higher wages and better working conditions. This suggestion is in line with the main themes of the various efficiency wage models (Yellen 1984; Katz 1986; Lang and Dickens 1994). Most efficiency wage models assume that higher wages lead to higher profits. This assumption is based on the assumption that labor productivity and output depend on wages. In efficiency wage models, one of the intermediate factors by which wages influence labor productivity and output is the quit rate. In other words, efficiency wage models suggest that higher wages increase labor productivity and output by reducing workers' quits.

A second sociological question was posed in Chapter 1: How is the value that workers place on more desirable transition outcomes modified by individual and structural factors? To answer this question, I make two assumptions.

First, workers who leave their current workplaces hope for more desirable transition outcomes to maximize socioeconomic gains. Second, workers who have acquired more material, intangible, or social assets at their current workplaces have a better chance of having more desirable transition outcomes. Specifically, more material assets (such as earnings) enable workers to have more means and time to find better destinations; more intangible assets (such as skills and knowledge that are related to workers' job performance) can help them to find workplaces providing higher wages and better working conditions; and workers with more social assets (such as networks of interpersonal ties) have the advantage of finding better workplaces more easily because the dominant way of matching individuals to employers is the use of interpersonal ties (Tilly and Tilly 1998: 140; Marsden and Gorman 2001).

The mechanism by which a more desirable transition outcome occurs, therefore, is that if an individual or structural characteristic contributes to acquiring more material, intangible, or social assets at workers' current workplaces, it increases the desirability of transition outcomes.

As discussed in Chapter 1, the above two sociological questions are related to two aspects of employment transitions, i.e., employment stability and the desirability of transition outcomes, constituting a two-stage process a worker goes through voluntarily or involuntarily. Therefore, theoretical models that this study will use to answer these questions can be regarded as a two-stage employment transition model.

In order to answer the second sociological question, I classify destinations of employment transitions as (1) entrepreneurship, (2) new employment in internal labor markets, (3) self-employment, (4) new employment in external labor markets, and (5) nonemployment. These are ordered from the most to the least desirable destinations for employees who leave their workplaces.

Entrepreneurs are employers hiring at least more than several workers to operate their business, and I assume that employees think of entrepreneurship as an opportunity to pursue the greatest economic success although it is usually difficult to become an entrepreneur (Casson 1982: 347).[1] Furthermore, I assume that entrepreneurship provides the best chance to improve working conditions, especially autonomy in work such as work flexibility, opportunities for creativity, and control over work.

The fact that entrepreneurship provides the best chance to increase autonomy in work has been pointed out by theories on entrepreneurship. The most influential theorist of entrepreneurship is arguably Schumpeter (Barreto 1989: 22-33; Martinelli 1994; Ripsas 1998; Swedberg 2000; Blaug 2000; Brouwer 2000). Schumpeter (1949, 1976) sees entrepreneurship as the key agent of economic development. According to him, an entrepreneur is an innovator who introduces new products, new methods of production, new markets, new sources of producer goods, or new organizations. Other aspects of the active role of entrepreneurship in economic activities have also been pointed out: Kirzner (1973) sees an entrepreneur as an arbitrageur who establishes market equilibrium by being alert to and capturing unnoticed profit opportunities that already exist. According to Casson (1982: 23), "an entrepreneur is someone who specializes in taking judgmental decisions about the coordination of scarce resources."

We can say that these characterizations of entrepreneurship point to the fact that entrepreneurship involves the highest autonomy in work among all employment statuses. For employees who leave their workplaces, therefore, moving to entrepreneurship is more desirable than moving to any other destination, since entrepreneurship potentially provides the greatest economic success and the highest autonomy in work.

Nonemployment comprises unemployment, in which people do not work but search for jobs, and those out of the labor force. Generally speaking, nonemployment is the least desirable destination employees find themselves in once they leave their workplaces, because moving to nonemployment usually means the loss of income at least for a short period of time.

As will be discussed in more detail later in this chapter, internal labor markets are defined as labor markets where job ladders with entry port only at the bottom or with non-entry-port positions filled only by internal promotions exist, and external labor markets as labor markets where they do not exist. One of the key differences between the effects of internal labor markets and those of external labor markets is that wages are higher and working conditions are better in internal labor markets than in external labor markets. In other words, internal promotions on job ladders in internal labor markets are usually associated with increases in wages and improvements in working conditions. This is because employers in internal labor markets invest more in workers, anticipating that prospects of internal promotions on job ladders make workers more likely to stay with them, so that they can elicit higher productivity from workers in the long run. The self-employed consist of own account workers and employers hiring just a small number of workers.[2]

It is obvious that for employees who have left their workplaces, new employment in internal labor markets is more desirable than new employment in external labor markets. Self-employment falls between these two. This is because self-employment jobs are usually not as good as jobs in internal labor markets in terms of socio-economic status, earnings, and working conditions whereas workers in external labor markets are likely to regard self-employment as a desirable path that will allow them to pursue greater economic success outside their current employment relations. This is especially true in Korea that has a considerable self-employment sector, in large part consisting of the self-employed who do not hire any employees.

The existence of a considerable self-employment sector in Korea has tended to put pressure to lower wages of employees, especially employees in external labor markets. This is mainly because the self-employed and employees in external labor markets often compete with each other in the same economic sector. As mentioned above, external labor markets are characterized by the lack of job ladders. This means that external labor markets tend to develop in the economic sector that provides products and services based on simple and labor-intensive technologies. The self-employed also tend to provide the same kind of products and services because their capital and skills are limited due to the fact that they mainly work by themselves and their business is usually not entrepreneurial.

The existence of a considerable self-employment sector has also enabled Korean workers in external labor markets to find self-employment jobs easily, and has encouraged workers who have acquired some amount of material, intangible, or social assets during their employment to quit their jobs and pursue greater economic success as the self-employed. Employers in external labor markets usually do not provide incentives to keep workers because workers in external labor markets, in which simple and labor-intensive technologies are predominant, are easily replaceable. Furthermore, only very limited forms of public support are available for the elderly in Korea, so that many workers in external labor markets regard self-employment as one of the most important means of providing for their old age (Kim et al. 1999: 62).

One way of justifying the above ranking of employment transition outcomes in terms of their desirability for workers is to look at differences in socio-economic status, income, and working hours by employment status. Table 3-1 shows typical examples of working people for each one of the employment statuses mentioned above except nonemployment. Tables 3-2 and 3-3 present some statistics relevant to socio-economic status, income, and working hours by employment status for working people in Korea in 1996. More specifically, Table 3-2 presents the subjective appraisal of own income and social status classes, and Table 3-3 actual average annual income and average weekly working hours.

The statistics in Table 3-2 show that there are few differences in the subjective appraisal of own income and social status classes between entrepreneurs and workers in internal labor markets and between the self-employed and workers in external labor markets. One might say, therefore, that the above way of ranking employment statuses in terms of their desirability for workers can only be partially supported.

The statistics about the actual average annual income in Table 3-3, however, imply that entrepreneurship and self-employment are more desirable than employment in internal labor markets and employment in external labor markets, respectively. It is true that the continuous annual average income is smaller for employment in internal labor markets than for self-employment. But the cate-

Table 3-1. Examples of Working People for Each Employment Status

Employment Status	Examples
Entrepreneurship	Employers hiring five or more employees.* Owners of medium- to large-sized restaurants, supermarkets, groceries, bookstores, etc. Employers of private firms.
Employment in Internal Labor Markets	Employees who have been promoted or have the prospect of being promoted. Male white-collar workers who have graduated from college.
Self-Employment	Own account workers.** Employers hiring less than five employees. Owners of small restaurants, groceries, bookstores, etc. Street peddlers selling various kinds of miscellaneous goods on their own.
Employment in External Labor Markets	Employees who neither have been promoted nor have the prospect of being promoted. Female blue-collar workers who have not graduated from college.

* In the data used in this study, 69 employees, each of whom had one work spell, became entrepreneurs, and only 11.59 percent of them hired 30 or more employees.
** In the data used in this study, there were 561 transitions from employment to self-employment, and 72.91 percent of such transitions involved employees' becoming own account workers.

gorical annual income is greater for the former. Besides, one can say that working conditions are better for the former because workers in internal labor markets work much less hours than the self-employed. We can say, therefore, that we have some convincing evidence supporting the claim that for Korean employees, employment in internal labor markets is more desirable than self-employment.

In this chapter, I present theoretical models on employment transitions. Some of the most important individual and structural factors influencing employment transitions I consider in this study are labor market structure, human capital, gender and gender-related factors, organization-level factors, and chronological time. In order to present theoretical models on the influences of these factors on employment transitions, I review and expand on previous studies and research on the subject, and present my expectations about the effects of each factor and of interactions between labor market structure and each of the other factors on employment transition patterns.

Table 3-2. Subjective Appraisal of Own Income and Social Status Classes by Employment Status: Korea, 1996

Employment Status	Subjective Appraisal				% (N = 2,618)
	Own Income Class*		Own Social Status Class*		
	Mean	Median	Mean	Median	
Entrepreneurship	4.82	5	4.76	5	2.59
Employment in Internal Labor Markets	4.58 (0.143)[†]	5	4.64 (0.497)[†]	5	26.02
Self-Employment	4.35 (0.005)[†]	5	4.28 (<0.0005)[†]	4	27.11
Employment in External Labor Markets	4.24 (0.181)[†]	4	4.25 (0.701)[†]	4	44.28

Source: East Asia Social Survey on People's Work Life: South Korea (See the Data Source section of Chapter 4).
* From 1 to 10; 1 is the lowest class and 10 is the highest class (See Questions e151 and e152 in Appendix A).
[†] The difference between this figure and the figure in the one-row-above cell in the same column is statistically significant at this p-level.
Note: All statistics are weighted by the variable designed to make the sample nationally representative (See the Data Source section of Chapter 4).

Labor Market Structure

The central purpose of this project is to investigate the effects of labor market structure on employment transition patterns in Korea. The labor market is the space where workers' labor power is exchanged for financial reward, so that labor market structure refers to the way in which such exchanges occur.

This study focuses on two aspects of the way in which these exchanges occur: (1) the relationship between jobs, and (2) the way in which workers are matched to jobs. First, the relationship between jobs in a labor market can be either hierarchical or horizontal in terms of authority given to occupants of each job; it is also characterized by whether or not jobs are differentiated based on levels of skills and knowledge. Second, an organization matches workers and jobs by external recruitments, internal movements, or some combination of the two. Theories of internal labor markets help specify these aspects of labor market structure systematically.

Doeringer and Piore (1985: 1-2) define an internal labor market as "an administrative unit, such as a manufacturing plant, within which the pricing and

Table 3-3. Actual Annual Income and Working Hours by Employment Status: Korea, 1996

| Em- ployment Status | Annual Income Including Tax* (10,000 Korean won) | | | | | | Weekly Working Hours | |
| | Continuous | | | Categorical | | | | |
	Mean	Me- dian	% ($n =$ 1,673)	Mo- dal Cate gory	Cate gory Con- tain- ing Me- dian	% ($n =$ 782)	Mean	% ($n =$ 2,531)
Entre- preneur- ship	2686.54	3000	2.67	3000 – 4999	2100 – 2999	3.24	57.87	2.65
Employ- ment in Internal Labor Markets	1866.63 $(<0.0005)^\dagger$	1800	31.66	1500 – 2099	1500 – 2099	20.20	50.91 $(<0.0005)^\dagger$	26.54
Self- Employ- ment	2026.11 $(0.021)^\dagger$	2000	23.83	900 – 1499	900 – 1499	41.76	64.24 $(<0.0005)^\dagger$	26.17
Employ- ment in External Labor Markets	1554.82 $(<0.0005)^\dagger$	1500	41.85	900 – 1499	900 – 1499	34.80	55.84 $(<0.0005)^\dagger$	44.64

Source: Same as in Table 3-2.

* Respondents answered only one question out of the question about their continuous income and the question about their categorical income (See Questions c111 and c11av1 in Appendix A).

† The difference between this figure and the figure in the one-row-above cell in the same column is statistically significant at this p-level.

Note: All statistics are weighted in the same way as in Table 3-2.

allocation of labor is governed by a set of administrative rules and procedures." Althauser and Kalleberg (1981: 130) further specify internal labor market structure as "(*a*) a job ladder, with (*b*) entry port only at the bottom and (*c*) movement up this ladder."

A job ladder is a hierarchy of jobs requiring different levels of skills and knowledge. It does not necessarily entail entry port only at the bottom or movement up this ladder, i.e., internal promotions on this ladder. This is because it is possible that each position on a hierarchy of jobs requiring different levels of skills and knowledge can be filled with workers outside an organization.

The second criterion of internal labor markets, entry port only at the bottom, does not necessarily imply the existence of a job ladder, for entry port can also be limited to the bottom of a hierarchy of jobs with the same level of skills and knowledge; it should, however, imply movement up a hierarchy of jobs with either different levels or the same level of skills and knowledge. The purpose of limiting entry port only at the bottom, therefore, is to facilitate internal promotions (Althauser and Kalleberg 1981: 130).

The third criterion, internal promotions on a hierarchy of jobs, do not necessarily imply the existence of a job ladder because they can occur on a hierarchy of jobs with the same level of skills and knowledge; but they must entail entry port only at the bottom if every position except the position at the bottom of a hierarchy of jobs is filled only by internal promotions.

In sum, in order to define a labor market as an internal labor market, we need to identify first a hierarchy of jobs requiring different levels of skills and knowledge, then either (1) entry port only at the bottom of this hierarchy of jobs or (2) each position, excluding the position at the bottom, filled only by internal promotions on this hierarchy of jobs. In this study, therefore, an internal labor market (ILM) is defined as a labor market that has a job ladder, i.e., a hierarchy of jobs requiring different levels of skills and knowledge, with entry port only at the bottom or with internal promotions as the only way of filling every position except the entry port position, and an external labor market (ELM) as a labor market that does not.[3]

Since the effects of organization-level characteristics on employment transition patterns are also explored in this study, it is important to note that the boundaries between internal and external labor markets do not always correspond to those between organizations. In other words, internal and external labor markets can exist within an organization at the same time. For example, Korean banks employed "general bank clerks" and "female bank clerks" until 1993 (*The Chosun Ilbo*. September 17, 1993). Most general bank clerks were males and had opportunities for internal promotions whereas female bank clerks rarely had such opportunities regardless of their completed level of schooling. In this case, a Korean bank had internal and external labor markets at the same time: General bank clerks belonged to an internal labor market, and female bank clerks comprised an external labor market.

Other theorists suggest different criteria for internal labor markets. For example, Ryan (1981: 15-6) suggests that the criteria of job ladders and opportunities for internal promotions cannot be the appropriate criteria for internal labor markets, maintaining that the key feature of internal labor markets is that employees in internal labor markets enjoy better working conditions than those in external labor markets. But this suggestion—like the suggestions that associate internal labor markets with higher wages, more stable employment, the existence of seniority, and so on—actually speaks to the *effects* of internal labor markets rather than the *structure* of internal labor markets itself.

There has been some confusion in theories on internal labor markets because they often do not distinguish between the structure of internal labor markets, the mechanisms by which that structure emerges, and the effects that structure causes (Kim et al. 1999: 3). This confusion may lead to further confusion in empirical research in that one may be tempted to define internal labor markets using indicators already related to some dependent variables. For example, if employment stability is used as a criterion for internal labor markets, studying the effect of internal labor markets on employment stability will be a tautology. To avoid this kind of problem, it is necessary to define internal labor markets in terms of their structure first.

Internal labor market theory is an important part of a broader theory that is referred to as dual labor market theory or segmented labor market theory. According to segmented labor market theory, labor markets are segmented by various factors such as job characteristics, class, gender, and race (Wallace and Kalleberg 1981: 91; Ryan 1981: 16-8). Segmented labor market theory suggests that workers are clustered into primary and secondary labor markets in terms of desirability of job characteristics. Job characteristics include "the skill and training involved, job security and attachment, opportunities for advancement, breadth of job definition, level of worker participation in decisions, and compensation" (Tilly and Tilly 1994: 294). Among these characteristics, the above discussion about internal labor markets deals with the skill and training, opportunities for advancement, and breadth of job definition. If we focus on the way in which job positions are filled in each unit of labor markets, primary and secondary labor markets can be referred to as internal and external labor markets, respectively. Therefore, we can say that internal labor market theory that is considered in this study represents an important part of segmented labor market theory.

Segmented labor market theory is closely related to dual economy theory since it is suggested that variables significantly causing labor market segmentations include "market concentration, economic scale, profits, process of production, capital intensity, economic growth and the expansion of markets, and the role of the state" (Wallace and Kalleberg 1981: 91).

Some studies demonstrate that segmented labor market theory and dual economy theory can appropriately explain the Korean labor market. For example, Deyo (1989: 8, 167-201) shows that the Korean labor market has been segmented between light and heavy industries: The labor-intensive and export-oriented light industry has disproportionately attracted young, low-skilled, and female workers. In contrast, the capital-intensive, heavy industry has largely recruited more skilled and male workers. As a result, workers in light industry have been disadvantaged in terms of wages and workings conditions. Similarly, Koo (1990) points out that because female workers have been disproportionately concentrated in the labor-intensive export industries and male workers in heavy and chemical industries, the rate of proletarianization caused by the rapid labor-intensive industrialization in the 1960s and 1970s was faster among female workers than among male workers in Korea.[4]

Only a few studies have been done on the effect of internal labor markets on employment stability. Using the personnel records of a large American insurance company from 1970 through 1978, Petersen and Spilerman (1990) demonstrate that the promotion rate is negatively associated with the separation rate. From this result, I suggest that employment stability is higher in internal labor markets than in external labor markets, for we generally observe more promotions in internal labor markets than in external labor markets. Yoo (1996) shows that internal labor markets reduce labor mobility in Korea when three indicators for an internal labor market are met: screening devices for hiring, internal promotion ladders, and high proportion of new entry at the bottom level.

On the basis of the conceptualizations of internal labor markets and the results of the studies presented above, this project argues that Korean employees in internal labor markets show higher employment stability than their counterparts in external labor markets. I suggest that the underlying mechanism that translates experience in internal labor markets into higher employment stability is as follows. Employers in internal labor markets believe that the efficient operation of job ladders contributes to increased profits by increasing labor productivity. Workers in internal labor markets believe that more promotion opportunities that job ladders provide lead to increases in wages and improvements in working conditions. Employers in internal labor markets try to enhance the efficiency of job ladders to increase profits, and workers in internal labor markets try to take advantage of promotion opportunities to earn higher wages and work under better working conditions. On the part of employers, reducing employment transitions by providing higher wages and better working conditions for workers in higher positions on job ladders is helpful to the efficient operation of job ladders. On the part of employees, staying at their current workplaces as long as possible is necessary for taking advantage of promotion opportunities job ladders provide. As a result, employment relationships are more stable in internal labor markets where job ladders exist than in external labor markets where they do not.

This project also argues that the Korean employees in internal labor markets show more desirable transition outcomes than their counterparts in external labor markets. I suggest that the underlying mechanism that translates experience in internal labor markets into more desirable transition outcomes is as follows. Promotions on job ladders in internal labor markets enable workers who are promoted to accumulate more material, intangible, or social assets that lead them to more desirable workplaces once they leave their current workplaces compared to the structure of external labor markets. Material, intangible, or social assets acquired at the current workplace are especially valuable for transitions to entrepreneurship because entrepreneurship usually requires a larger amount of such assets than other destinations.

The expectations presented in this section about the influences of labor market structure on employment transition patterns in Korea can be summarized as follows.

- **Workers in internal labor markets show higher employment stability and more desirable transition outcomes than workers in external labor markets.**

Human Capital

The effects of internal labor markets on employment transition patterns are seen more clearly when other factors that also affect employment transition patterns are controlled. One set of such factors is workers' human capital.

Human capital can be classified into general human capital and firm-specific human capital (Becker 1993). General human capital is the kind of human capital that can be used to increase workers' productivity regardless of their workplace. In contrast, firm-specific human capital is the kind of human capital that is of use only at a specific workplace. General on-the-job training, formal or informal, and formal education are measures by which workers acquire general human capital. Workers acquire firm-specific human capital mainly through firm-specific on-the-job training, formal or informal.

Mincer (1962) shows that in the United States, (1) a higher level of formal education is associated with more on-the-job training, and (2) more on-the-job training is associated with lower rates of turnover plus unemployment, i.e., higher employment stability. Mincer and Jovanovic (1981), Altonji and Shakotko (1986), Topel (1986), and Dar (1993) demonstrate that in the United States, firm-specific human capital accumulation is negatively associated with inter-firm mobility when job tenure is used as a proxy for firm-specific human capital. Using work history data for 30- to 39-year-old male wage laborers in the nonagricultural sector in the United States in 1968, Tuma (1985) shows the relationship between general and firm-specific human capital and reward changes after inter-firm transitions: (1) Education and job tenure are positively associated with increases in occupational prestige and the wage rate. (2) Education and job tenure are negatively associated with decreases in occupational prestige and the wage rate. Theoretical models underlying these empirical findings can be specified as follows.

Employers do not give a wage premium to employees with general human capital in order to reduce their turnover because it is employees that have to pay the cost of acquiring general human capital (Becker 1993: 45). Although employers do not try to reduce the turnover of employees with general human capital, it is expected that employees with more general human capital show higher employment stability, for employment stability increases as the expected gains from a job match increase (Tuma 1985). Expected gains rise with increases in the skill level of a job, which is positively associated with an employee's education level. Therefore, employment stability increases as an employee's education level increases. In other words, employees with higher education level are more likely to stay at the current workplace because they expect more gains at the current workplace on the basis of their higher productivity.

Employers try to reduce the turnover of employees with firm-specific human capital by giving them a wage premium because they pay part of firm-specific on-the-job training cost (Becker 1993: 45). Since firm-specific human capital is valuable only at the current workplace, workers with more firm-specific human capital want to stay at their current workplaces as long as possible, and want to increase their wages and improve their working conditions.

This discussion about the behaviors of both employers and workers leads to the expectation that workers with more human capital, general or firm-specific, show higher employment stability than workers with less human capital in Korea.

Workers with more human capital, general or firm-specific, also have more chances of accumulating material, intangible, or social assets at their current workplaces that help them move to better workplaces than workers with less human capital. This is because the former (1) earn more wages for the reasons mentioned above, (2) have higher levels of skills and knowledge, and (3) make more social relations during the time they acquire more human capital. I suggest, therefore, that workers with more human capital have more desirable transition outcomes than workers with less human capital in Korea.

An investigation of an interaction between labor market structure and human capital will show whether or not internal labor market structure intensifies the influences of human capital on employment transition patterns in Korea. The behaviors of both employers and workers contribute to the effects of an interaction between labor market structure and human capital as follows.

The degree to which workers with more human capital are more productive than workers with less human capital is higher in internal labor markets than in external labor markets. The tasks of higher positions on a job ladder in an internal labor market are generally more complex and firm-specific. In order for a job ladder to operate efficiently, therefore, higher positions on a job ladder need to be filled with workers with more human capital, especially firm-specific human capital. Consequently, employers want to fill higher positions on a job ladder with workers with more human capital in order to make the tasks of higher positions handled more efficiently and workers in lower positions supervised more effectively. At the same time, workers with more human capital want to stay on a job ladder as long as possible to take advantage of the more promotion opportunities given to them.

These behaviors of both employers and workers with more human capital make workers with more human capital more likely to move up a job ladder. I expect, therefore, that internal labor market structure intensifies the effect of human capital on employment stability. That is to say, I expect that the degree to which workers with more human capital show higher employment stability than workers with less human capital is higher in internal labor markets than in external labor markets in Korea.

The degree to which workers with more human capital accumulate more material, intangible, or social assets that are valuable to moving to better workplaces compared to workers with less human capital is higher in internal labor markets than in external labor markets. Higher positions on a job ladder in an internal labor market are filled with workers with more human capital who have already accumulated more material, intangible, or social assets that are valuable to moving to better workplaces even if they do not occupy higher positions upon their transfer. In other words, the advantages for workers with more human capital in terms of accumulating the above assets are greater in internal labor markets than in external labor markets. The following elaborates on this point.

First, higher positions on a job ladder provide workers in those positions with higher wages because employers regard those positions as more important to the efficient operation of the job ladder. This means that workers with more human capital in those positions accumulate even more material assets that help them move to better workplaces. Second, the fact that the tasks of higher positions on a job ladder are more complex enables workers with more human capital in those positions to attain even more intangible assets such as skills and knowledge that help them move to better workplaces. Third, higher positions on a job ladder provide workers in those positions with more chances of contacting people outside as well as inside their current workplaces. This means that workers with more human capital in those positions accumulate even more social assets such as social networks that provide them with more information on better jobs outside their current workplaces and help them get those jobs.

In sum, internal labor market structure intensifies the effect of human capital on the desirability of transition outcomes. I expect, therefore, that the degree to which workers with more human capital have more desirable transition outcomes than workers with less human capital is higher in internal labor markets than in external labor markets in Korea.

The expectations presented in this section about the influences of human capital and of an interaction between labor market structure and human capital on employment transition patterns in Korea can be summarized as follows.

- **Workers with more human capital show higher employment stability and more desirable transition outcomes than workers with less human capital.**
- **The above tendency is stronger in internal labor markets than in external labor markets.**

Gender

Gender and gender-related factors constitute another important set of factors that affects employment transition patterns. In general, institutional and cultural practices based on patriarchal values tend to discourage women from being employed or from getting jobs with high wages and prestige (Sokoloff 1980; Walby 1986; England 1992). In other words, women as a disadvantaged group in a society are liable to suffer from less stable employment and less desirable transition outcomes due to the existence of patriarchy.

This phenomenon is especially conspicuous in Korea where strong extended-family, patrilineal descent traditions, and the Confucian ideology on gender roles in society and economy exist (Brinton, Lee, and Parish 1995; Kim 1995; Lee 1998). In other words, patriarchy has created various kinds of institutional and customary restrictions against stable employment and desirable transition outcomes for Korean women. Some examples of such restrictions are marriage and childbirth that are related to family formations, childcare and housework that are mainly assumed by women, and disadvantages that Korean women usually face at the workplace in terms of recruitment, promotion, earnings, and working conditions.

Felmlee (1980) shows that for the young white women in the United States between 1968 and 1973, being married and having young preschool children increase the likelihood of leaving employment voluntarily and having negative employment transition outcomes, i.e., changing to a job with lower wages or socioeconomic status. Using the same data, Felmlee (1982) demonstrates that the probability of getting married decreases the probability of voluntary job shifts with different employers. This result may be closely related to the fact that marriage increases the likelihood of entering nonemployment involuntarily and decreases the likelihood of reentering employment. Some studies support this interpretation: Phang (1995) shows that for the young black and white women in the United States between 1968 and 1991, first marriage and first childbirth increase the probability of exiting from employment. Brinton, Lee, and Parish (1995) suggest that the "marriage bar" phenomenon, i.e., the phenomenon that employers preferred single women to married women in hiring employees, existed at an earlier time in the United States, Britain, and Ireland. Bai and Cho (1995) show that the major reasons for retirement of female workers from the labor market after marriage are pregnancy and childbirth in Kuala Lumpur, and pregnancy, childbirth, and domestic responsibilities in Bangkok and Manila. Tsuya, Bumpass, and Choe (2000) show that the presence of small children decreases the likelihood of married women's employment in the United States and Japan.

On the basis of the analysis of changes in the patterns of women's labor force participation rates in Korea during the period from 1960 to 1980, Park (1990) demonstrates that getting married and having young children are likely to decrease women's labor force participation rates. Chin (1995) shows that the number of preschool children is strongly and negatively related to married women's labor force participation in Korea. Brinton, Lee, and Parish (1995) show that in Korea, married women with children under two years of age are highly likely to be nonemployees. Other studies also demonstrate that in Korea, marriage, childbirth, childcare, and responsibilities for housework decrease the likelihood of employment for women (Bai and Cho 1995; Kim 1996; Yee 1996; Yu 1996; K. Kim 1999; Y. Kim 1999; Tsuya, Bumpass, and Choe 2000). These results imply that married Korean women with young children are more likely to suffer from unstable employment and undesirable outcomes of employment transitions than other types of workers.

In this study, I will compare Korean women with Korean men in order to explore the influences of the restrictions related to gender on employment transition patterns. This comparison will show that the above restrictions decrease employment stability and the desirability of transition outcomes for Korean women. Furthermore, since childcare and housework are largely assumed only by women in Korea, I will compare Korean women with few childcare and housework responsibilities to Korean women with greater childcare and housework responsibilities. This comparison will show that Korean women with few childcare and housework responsibilities are in more stable employment and have more desirable transition outcomes than Korean women with greater childcare and housework responsibilities.

The way in which gender influences employment stability in Korea can be specified as follows. Employers generally believe that compared to female workers, male workers are more productive because male workers are superior to female workers in mental and physical capacities and social skills. Employers, therefore, usually believe that male workers contribute more to increased profits than female workers. Consequently, employers more strongly want the employment of male workers to be continued than they want the employment of female workers to be continued.

Employers' belief in the higher productivity and greater contributions to increased profits on the part of male workers influences workers' expectations regarding employment stability. Male workers know that employers prefer them to female workers, and that they have more chances of stable employment than female workers. Consequently, compared to female workers, male workers are less likely to leave their current workplaces when they have chances of doing so.

On the basis of employers' belief and workers' expectations regarding employment stability of female workers, I suggest that male workers show higher employment stability than female workers in Korea.

Gender-related factors such as childcare and housework influence employment stability of female workers in Korea in a similar way to the way in which gender influences employment stability. Employers generally believe that female workers with greater childcare and housework responsibilities are less productive than female workers with few childcare and housework responsibilities because childcare and housework responsibilities hinder workers from concentrating on their work. Employers, therefore, usually believe that the latter contribute more to increased profits than the former. Consequently, employers more strongly want the employment of the latter to be continued.

Employers' belief in the higher productivity and greater contributions to increased profits on the part of female workers with few childcare and housework responsibilities influences female workers' expectations regarding employment stability. Female workers with few childcare and housework responsibilities know that employers prefer them to female workers with greater childcare and housework responsibilities, and that they have more chances of stable employment comparatively. Consequently, they are less likely to leave their current workplaces when they have chances of doing so.

On the basis of employers' belief and workers' expectations regarding employment stability of female workers, I suggest that female workers with few childcare and housework responsibilities show higher employment stability than female workers with greater childcare and housework responsibilities in Korea.

I argued above that employers believe that male workers and those with few childcare and housework responsibilities are more productive and make greater contributions to increased profits. On the basis of this belief, employers pay these workers higher wages and assign them jobs requiring a higher degree of skill and knowledge. Furthermore, institutional and customary practices based on patriarchal values tend to allow these types of workers to make social relations inside and outside the current workplace more easily.

These arguments imply that (1) compared to female workers, male workers accumulate more material, intangible, or social assets at the current workplace that help them move to better workplaces, and (2) compared to workers with greater childcare and housework responsibilities, workers with few childcare and housework responsibilities accumulate more of the same assets. I suggest, therefore, that in Korea, (1) male workers have more desirable transition outcomes than female workers, and (2) female workers with few childcare and housework responsibilities have more desirable transition outcomes than female workers with greater childcare and housework responsibilities.

An investigation of an interaction between labor market structure and gender will show how internal labor market structure affects discrimination against female workers in terms of employment stability and the desirability of transition outcomes in Korea.

Employers in internal labor markets generally believe that male workers contribute more to the efficient operation of job ladders than female workers because male workers are superior to female workers in mental and physical capacities and social skills. For this reason, employers believe that male workers make greater contributions to the efficient operation of job ladders in internal labor markets than in external labor markets. Employers in internal labor markets, consequently, pay higher wages to and provide better working conditions for male workers than female workers by promoting the former more frequently than the latter. Male workers believe that they have more chance of promotion on job ladders in internal labor markets than female workers, so that they are less likely to leave their current workplaces when they have chances of doing so. As a result, the degree to which male workers show higher employment stability than female workers is higher in internal labor markets than in external labor markets in Korea.

Since male workers are promoted more frequently on job ladders in internal labor markets, the degree to which male workers accumulate more material, intangible, or social assets needed for moving to better workplaces than female workers is higher in internal labor markets than in external labor markets. Therefore, the degree to which male workers show more desirable transition outcomes than female workers is higher in internal labor markets than in external labor markets in Korea.

Investigating an interaction between labor market structure and childcare and housework responsibility will show how internal labor market structure affects discrimination against female workers with greater childcare and housework responsibilities in terms of employment stability and the desirability of transition outcomes in Korea.

Employers in internal labor markets generally believe that female workers with childcare and housework responsibilities contribute less to the efficient operation of job ladders compared to female workers without these responsibilities because childcare and housework responsibilities hinder workers from concentrating on their work. For this reason, employers' belief in the greater contributions to the efficient operation of job ladders on the part of the latter is stronger in internal labor markets than in external labor markets. Employers in internal labor markets, consequently, pay higher wages to and provide better working conditions for female workers without childcare and housework responsibilities by promoting them more frequently. These female workers are aware that they have more chance of promotion on job ladders in internal labor markets than female workers with greater childcare and housework responsibilities, so that they are less likely to leave their current workplaces when they have chances of doing so. As a result, the degree to which they show higher employment stability is higher in internal labor markets than in external labor markets in Korea.

Female workers with few childcare and housework responsibilities are more frequently promoted on job ladders in internal labor markets than female workers with greater childcare and housework responsibilities. For this reason, the degree to which they accumulate more material, intangible, or social assets needed for moving to better workplaces is higher in internal labor markets than in external labor markets. Therefore, the degree to which they show more desirable transition outcomes is higher in internal labor markets than in external labor markets in Korea.

The expectations presented in this section about the influences of gender and gender-related factors and of interactions between labor market structure and these factors on employment transition patterns in Korea can be summarized as follows.

- **Male workers show higher employment stability and more desirable transition outcomes than female workers.**
- **Female workers with few childcare and housework responsibilities show higher employment stability and more desirable transition outcomes than female workers with greater childcare and housework responsibilities.**
- **The above tendencies are stronger in internal labor markets than in external labor markets.**

Organization-Level Characteristics

Another important set of factors, which affects employment transition patterns, is that of organization-level characteristics such as organizational size and unionism. One issue in investigating the influences of organizational size and unionism on employment transition patterns is whether or not these organization-level characteristics overlap with labor market structure.

In fact, some researchers tend to use large organizational size as a proxy for an internal labor market. However, we can find a significant number of internal labor markets in small- to medium-sized firms, too. This is especially the case in Korea where many small- to medium-sized firms have imitated large firms' administrative rules and procedures governing the decisions about labor price and labor allocations (Kim et al. 1999: 67).

Similarly, a significant number of labor unions have existed in external labor markets as well as in internal labor markets in Korea. One of the main reasons for this is that workers in labor-intensive industries, who have usually been in external labor markets, have played important roles in rapid economic development and consistent labor movements in Korea.

Using retrospective work history data, Carroll and Mayer (1986) show that organizational size reduces the likelihood of across-firm transitions in West Germany. Using the May 1979 Current Population Survey, Rebitzer (1986) demonstrates that employer size and plant size enhance employment stability in the United States. The way in which organizational size affects employment stability can be specified as follows.

Generally speaking, a high rate of workers' turnovers is costly for employers, since it results in higher cost of recruiting and training workers and hinders increasing profits through enhancing labor productivity. Employers, therefore, generally try to reduce workers' turnovers. But the degree to which employers try to reduce workers' turnovers depends on firm size. Large firms usually use more complicated technologies than small firms because they are usually able to utilize greater capital in production processes. More complicated technologies make administrative procedures for recruiting workers more complicated. The cost of recruiting workers, therefore, is higher for employers in large firms than for employers in small firms. More complicated technologies also make the cost of training workers higher. Therefore, a high rate of worker turnover is more costly for employers in large firms, so that employers in large firms are more likely to try to reduce worker turnover than employers in small firms.

The main means of reducing worker turnover is providing workers with higher wages and better working conditions. Compared to small organizations, large organizations can provide workers with higher wages and better working conditions because of their greater power in the product market and their way of personnel management. Large organizations have greater resources coming from their greater market power, which is bolstered by the fact that they are usually located in the industrial sectors such as the export industrial sector that show higher productivity. Having greater resources, then, large organizations can provide their employees with higher wages and better working conditions than small organizations. In large organizations, unlike in small organizations, personnel management is mainly based on administrative rules and procedures rather than on arbitrary decisions of supervisors because more complicated technologies are used in large organizations. Working conditions, therefore, are better in large organizations than in small organizations. As a result, workers in large organizations are more likely to want the current employment relationship to be continued in order to maintain their advantages over workers in small organizations in terms of wages and working conditions.

It is easier for workers to accumulate material or social assets in large organizations than in small organizations. Resources of large organizations generated from their greater market power are provided for their employees in the form of higher wages, so that employees in large organizations save more earnings that are useful for moving to better workplaces. Workers in large are useful for moving to better workplaces. Workers in large organizations have more chances of making social relations that help them move to better workplaces. As a result, workers in large organizations are more likely to move to better workplaces once they leave their current workplaces.

Whether or not an organization is publicly owned and managed is another important organizational characteristic. Public organizations usually have bureaucratic structures and do not always behave according to the rule of profit maximization. This is definitely the case in developing countries such as Korea, in which state agencies and public enterprises have been playing a more important role in economic activities than in underdeveloped or developed countries (Wade 1990; Woo 1991; Amsden 1992; Kim 1997). In this project, along with large private organizations, public organizations will be considered large organizations. Since the employer of public organizations is basically the state, even relatively small public organizations share similar internal structures (such as bureaucracy) with private large organizations.

Another important organization-level characteristic considered in this study is whether an organization is unionized. Blau and Kahn (1983) demonstrate that for both younger and older American males in 1969, union membership reduces permanent separations. The mechanisms by which unionism affects employment transition patterns can be specified as follows.

There are two important effects of labor unions in the labor market: the union wage effect and the collective voice effect. These two effects influence employment transition patterns.

The union wage effect refers to the fact that labor unions can increase wages above competitive levels (Freeman and Medoff 1984: 6-7). Labor unions usually exist in noncompetitive industries, so that through the collective bargaining process, they can make the employer increase wages without making the competitiveness of the firm threatened. In other words, labor unions' bargaining power based on their members' solidarity causes the union wage effect. Because of this union wage effect, workers in unionized organizations are more likely to want to stay at their current workplaces than workers in nonunionized organizations.

The collective voice effect of unionism refers to the fact that a labor union makes it easier for its members to communicate with management, so that union members can more easily discuss with management working conditions that they think should be changed (Freeman and Medoff 1984: 7-8). Because of this collective voice effect, unionized workers are less likely to leave their current workplaces than nonunionized workers when there are complaints about working conditions.

Generally speaking, however, employers are not eager to keep unionized workers. Freeman and Medoff (1984: 162-90) show that labor unions generally increase productivity, have no influence on the profits of competitive firms, and decrease the profits of noncompetitive firms in the United States. In most cases, however, it is not easy for employers to fire unionized workers. Unionism prevents employers not only from firing unionized workers arbitrarily but also from hiring nonunionized workers easily. Furthermore, as Freeman and Medoff (1984: 186) point out, the decreased profits for noncompetitive firms are actually monopoly profits, so that noncompetitive firms can still enjoy higher profitability over competitive firms despite the decreased profits caused by unionism. Employers, therefore, have few means to fire unionized workers and still fewer means to avoid unionism that already exists.

The union wage effect also enables workers in unionized organizations to save more earnings that help them move to better workplaces. I expect, therefore, that workers in unionized organizations have more desirable transition outcomes than workers in nonunionized organizations.

The discussion on the effects of organization-level characteristics on employment transition patterns so far can be summarized as follows. First, employers and workers in large organizations are more likely to want the current employment relationship to be continued than their counterparts in small organizations, and workers in unionized organizations are more likely to want the current employment relationship to be continued than workers in nonunionized organizations. I expect, therefore, that large organizational size and unionism increase employment stability in Korea.

Second, it is easier for workers to accumulate material or social assets in large organizations and material assets in unionized organizations than in small organizations and in nonunionized organizations, respectively. Material or social assets help workers move to better workplaces. I expect, therefore, that large organizational size and unionism increase the desirability of transition outcomes in Korea.

In this study, interactions of labor market structure with organizational size and unionism will be explored to show whether or not internal labor market structure modifies the influences of organizational size and unionism on employment transition patterns in Korea.

I argued above that (1) more complicated technologies and greater market power of large organizations increase employment stability, and (2) greater market power of large organizations and more chances of making social relations in large organizations increase the desirability of transition outcomes. I expect that the effects of organizational size on employment transition patterns are stronger in internal labor markets than in external labor markets in Korea for three reasons.

First, firms with job ladders have more complicated technologies since most positions on job ladders require different kinds of skills and knowledge of workers. Second, firms with job ladders usually make more profits and have greater market power on the basis of the greater efficiency of their work organizations. Third, in firms with job ladders, workers have more chances of making social relations with other higher-ranking workers who have more material or social resources helpful in moving on to better work positions elsewhere.

I argued above that (1) workers' greater bargaining power and ease of communication between workers and management in unionized firms increase employment stability, and (2) workers' greater bargaining power in unionized firms increases the desirability of transition outcomes through the union wage effect. I expect that the effects of unionism on employment transition patterns are stronger in internal labor markets than in external labor markets in Korea for two reasons.

First, higher positions on job ladders require workers to have higher levels of skills and knowledge, so that workers in internal labor markets are overall more valuable to employers than workers in external labor markets. Workers in internal labor markets, therefore, have greater bargaining power against employers than workers in external labor markets. Second, workers in higher positions on job ladders can communicate with management more easily because they are considered to play a more important role in the operation of job ladders. Consequently, workers in internal labor markets can communicate with management more easily than workers in external labor markets.

In sum, I expect that internal labor market structure intensifies the influences of organizational size and unionism on employment transition patterns in Korea.

The expectations presented in this section about the influences of organization-level characteristics and of interactions between labor market structure and organization-level characteristics on employment transition patterns in Korea can be summarized as follows.

- **Workers in large organizations show higher employment stability and more desirable transition outcomes than workers in small organizations.**
- **Workers in unionized organizations show higher employment stability and more desirable transition outcomes than workers in nonunionized organizations.**
- **The above tendencies are stronger in internal labor markets than in external labor markets.**

Time

In Chapter 2, I argued the following. (1) The effects of time on employment transition patterns consist of the effects of changes in the economic structure and the effects of changes in the state's labor market policies. (2) The effects of changes in the economic structure can be specified as the effects of industrial deepening. (3) The effects of changes in the state's labor market policies can be specified as the effects of partial relaxation of strict state labor controls. (4)

These two kinds of effects increased employment stability and the desirability of transition outcomes in Korea after 1986. On the basis of these arguments, I will explore in this section whether or not the degree of the influences of labor market structure on both employment stability and the desirability of transition outcomes changed in Korea during industrialization.

Changes in the economic structure and changes in the state's labor market policies have affected the way in which an internal labor market keeps its workers and enables them to accumulate material, intangible, or social assets that help them move to better workplaces in Korea.

Generally speaking, internal promotions on a job ladder in an internal labor market accompany increases in wages and improvements in working conditions—both are necessary for employers to keep their employees within their firms. Workers in an internal labor market, however, will exit the workplace and get new jobs at other workplaces if they find those new jobs more desirable to them in terms of wages and working conditions. This situation is more likely when a job ladder in an internal labor market has not matured, i.e., it is relatively short and simple. This is because a short and simple job ladder provides less opportunities for internal promotions, consequently, less opportunities for increases in wages and improvements in working conditions. A short and simple job ladder also discourages workers from accumulating material, intangible, or social assets that help them move to more desirable workplaces.

Therefore, the degree to which an internal labor market has advantages over an external labor market in keeping its workers and allowing them to accumulate material, intangible, or social assets that help them move to better workplaces depends on the degree of maturation of a job ladder in an internal labor market. In the context of Korea, two aspects of time, i.e., changes in the economic structure and changes in the state's labor market policies, have significantly influenced the degree of maturation of a given job ladder in an internal labor market. I suggest, therefore, that these two aspects of time influenced the degree of the effects of labor market structure on employment transition patterns in Korea during industrialization. This suggestion will be supported by investigating interactions of labor market structure with changes in the economic structure and changes in the state's labor market policies.

First, it is shown in Chapter 2 that Korea achieved rapid industrial deepening during industrialization. The increase in the relative importance of heavy industry in the entire economy, which has been evident since the onset of Korea's rapid industrialization, implies considerable maturation of the job ladder in the Korean internal labor market. This is because (1) jobs in heavy industry, having more complex technologies and work organizations than light industry, usually require higher levels of skills and knowledge of workers than jobs in light industry, and (2) higher levels of skills and knowledge are conducive to maturation of job ladders in internal labor markets. I suggest, therefore, that the increase in the relative importance of heavy industry in the entire economy raised the degree to which internal labor market structure increased both employment stability and the desirability of transition outcomes in Korea during industrialization.

Second, as discussed in Chapter 2, due to strict labor control policies by the state, the rates of increases in wages were generally lower than the rates of increases in labor productivity and were mainly based on individual-level rather than structure-level factors before 1987. Beginning in 1987, however, partial relaxation of strict labor control policies due to strong political challenges from students and workers enabled structure-level factors (including the job ladder) to play a more important role in determining wage levels. This facilitated considerable maturation of the job ladder in the Korean internal labor market. I suggest, therefore, that partial relaxation of strict labor control policies raised the degree to which internal labor market structure increased both employment stability and the desirability of transition outcomes in Korea.

On the basis of the above discussion on interactions of labor market structure with changes in the economic structure and changes in the state's labor market policies, I suggest that in Korea, the degree to which internal labor market structure increased both employment stability and the desirability of transition outcomes was lower before 1987 than in 1987-1996.

The expectations presented in this section about the effects of an interaction between labor market structure and time on employment transition patterns in Korea can be summarized as follows.

- **The tendency that workers in internal labor markets show higher employment stability and more desirable transition outcomes than workers in external labor markets was stronger after 1986 than before 1987.**

Conclusion

In Chapters 2 and 3, I suggested that differences in employment transition patterns among Korean workers have been affected by labor market structure, human capital, gender and gender-related factors, organizational size, unionism, and time, which consists of changes in the economic structure and changes in the state's labor market policies. Special attention was given to the role of internal labor market structure in influencing employment transition patterns by considering interactions between labor market structure and each of the other factors. One of the main implications of the discussion on the effects of such interactions is that internal labor market structure has increased differences in employment transition patterns among Korean workers. In other words, internal labor market structure has increased employment stability and the desirability of transition outcomes for workers who already have had greater resources and have been in various kinds of more favorable positions in the labor market.

Theories in this chapter about the influences of the factors mentioned above on employment transition patterns in Korea have largely been based on theories and research that have been developed and performed in the context of Western countries. One of the important objectives of this project is to explore whether or not theories based on situations in Western countries are valid in explaining employment transition patterns in Korea, a country that has experienced rapid industrialization during the last four decades.

Theories in this chapter about the effects of gender and gender-related factors have been based on theories and research that have been developed and performed in the contexts of several developing and advanced industrial countries. This study will show whether these wide-spread effects of gender and gender-related factors are also in operation in Korea.

Theories on the effects of time have been developed in this chapter because it is thought that time represents some of unique factors related to Korea's exceptionally rapid industrialization and drastic political changes. Therefore, along with the effects of factors that Korea has had in common with Western countries and other developing countries, the effects of factors unique to Korea will be explored in this study.

In short, this study aims to investigate whether both common factors found in a variety of countries and factors unique to Korea have concurrently influenced employment transition patterns in Korea.

Notes

1 In this study, I define entrepreneurs as employers hiring at least five workers because I assume that the business of employers hiring less than five workers is usually for subsistence rather than entrepreneurial.

2 Employers hiring less than five workers are considered the self-employed in this study for the reason mentioned in the preceding footnote.

3 Unless otherwise specified, a job ladder means a job ladder with entry port only at the bottom or with internal promotions as the only way of filling every position except the entry port position in this study. The most important subtypes of an internal labor market that have been proposed so far are a firm internal labor market and an occupational internal labor market. If an internal labor market exists within a firm, it is called an enterprise market (Doeringer and Piore 1985: 2-3) or a firm internal labor market. If an internal labor market exists within an occupation, it is called a craft market (ibid.: 3-4) or an occupational internal labor market. Occupational internal labor markets, however, will not be considered in this study, for they have been an exception in Korea (Jung 1992: 221-2). Internal labor markets, therefore, refer to firm internal labor markets in this study.

4 Koo (1990: 669) defines proletarianization as "an increase in the number of people who lack control over the means of production and survive by selling their labor power."

4 Research Methods on Employment Transitions

Introduction

This project needs two kinds of data: data for the analysis of factors influencing employment stability and data for the analysis of factors influencing the desirability of transition outcomes.

One can assume that how long a worker stays at a workplace influences whether or not he or she leaves his or her workplace. Event history data contain information on the occurrence and timing of events per some time unit (Allison 1995: 1-5). In order to analyze appropriately factors that have influenced employment stability, we need event history data containing workers' work histories, i.e., times of employment transitions.

It is true that one can analyze factors that have influenced employment stability without using information on the occurrence of an employment transition per time unit. In this case, however, one has to disregard information on workers who still have not left their workplaces, which may cause significant biases.

The appropriate data should also include information on various time-constant and time-varying factors that may have influenced employment stability over time. Gender and level of completed education are examples of time-constant factors, and marital status, number of children, calendar year at a workplace, and the characteristics of a job, a workplace, and an employment relationship are examples of time-varying factors.

In short, the appropriate data should incorporate information needed for creating time-varying dependent variables and both time-constant and time-varying independent variables. The time unit of time-varying dependent and independent variables in the data should be precise enough to capture all significant changes in relevant variables.

The data for investigating factors that have influenced the desirability of transition outcomes should include information on the relevant variables recorded at the times of employment transitions. This kind of data can easily be created from the event history data for investigating factors that have influenced employment stability: Among the observations in the event history data, only the observations at the times of employment transitions should be kept.

In this chapter, I will describe the source of the data for this study, the method of transforming the original data into the data suitable for this study, the methods of analysis, and the operationalization of dependent and independent variables. The expected effects of the independent variables and important descriptive statistics of the sample will also be shown.

Data Source

The data that will be analyzed in this study are from the East Asia Social Survey on People's Work Life: South Korea. The questionnaire of the East Asia Social Survey on People's Work Life (hereafter the East Asia Social Survey) was jointly designed by the Institute for Social Development Studies at Yonsei University in Korea, the Academia Sinica in Taiwan, and the National Opinion Research Center associated with the University of Chicago in the United States. The East Asia Social Survey was conducted in Korea by Hyondae Research Institute in December 1996 through early 1997, and in Taiwan by the Academia Sinica during July 1996.

The Korean sample of the East Asia Social Survey is a representative sample of the entire nation except Jeju Island. The population was men and women aged 25 to 60 in 1996. The proportions of sexes, age cohorts, and regions for the sample were decided based on the population proportions by sex, age cohort, and region that appeared in the 1990 Census of Population and Housing by the National Statistical Office. The sample consists of two sub-samples. In the first 2,567 respondent sub-sample, the proportions of self-employed people and sales and service workers are higher than their national proportions; the other sub-sample contains 1,003 respondents and is nationally representative. In order to make the entire 3,570 respondent sample nationally representative, a weighting variable was created as described in Appendix B.

The sampling method was a multistage stratified cluster sampling. The sampling design is described in detail in Appendix C. The survey method was face-to-face individual interview conducted by trained interviewers. The questionnaire included demographic, current job and workplace characteristics, and retrospective work histories. Relevant questions used in this study are shown in Appendix A.

The fact that the data contain retrospective work histories reported by respondents may influence the validity of results of the analysis. In general, self-reporting is subject to the intentional or unintentional distortion of facts. This problem can be more serious when respondents are asked to recall their past work histories, for their inaccurate memories can lead to reporting inaccurate work histories (Tuma 1972: 105; Carroll and Mayer 1986: 326). Unfortunately, there is no clear way of getting around this kind of problem. Results of the analysis in this study, therefore, need to be cautiously interpreted as having potential biases caused by the method of data collection.

It is essential to incorporate appropriate time-varying variables in event history data in order to investigate factors that have influenced employment stability and the desirability of transition outcomes over time. As will be shown later in this chapter, however, some variables included in the event history data are not completely time-varying. Specifically, the characteristics of organizations are not completely time-varying. Questions about such characteristics in the questionnaire of the East Asia Social Survey were asked about an entire work spell, not about each year of a work spell. To some degree, this weakness is inevitable for this kind of retrospective event history data, since it is usually difficult for a respondent to recall each year of his or her entire work history, especially when he or she is relatively old. This weakness of the data makes it difficult to regard the data as ideal event history data. However, as will be argued later in this chapter, I argue that the seriousness of this weakness will be lessened if we acknowledge that it is unusual for the characteristics of organizations to change every year during a worker's employment.

Another weakness of the data is that their time unit—a year—is coarse; the data do not show information on more than one employment period that occurred in the same year. This weakness decreases the ability of this study to investigate factors that have influenced employment transition patterns over time as accurately as possible. As mentioned above, however, this weakness is inevitable for this kind of retrospective work history data to some degree, for it is generally very difficult for a respondent to recall his or her entire work history accurately if the time unit is less than a year.

Despite these weaknesses, of all available data, the data used in this study come closest to the ideal data suitable for analyzing factors that have influenced employment transition patterns in Korea over time. If appropriate methods are used, therefore, this study of the East Asia Social Survey data will be able to investigate factors that have influenced employment transition patterns in Korea over time more appropriately than any other study of the subject that analyzed other data.

Creating Data

The observation unit and the time unit of the original data from the East Asia Social Survey are an individual and a year, respectively. To investigate factors that have influenced employment stability, the original data will be transformed into event history data, the observation unit of which is a person-year.

The unit of analysis for the event history data is a work spell, i.e., a spell in which a worker stays at the same workplace continuously. Calendar years for the work spells range from 1949 to 1996. If two or more work spells are overlapped, only the work spell with the longest average weekly working hours will be kept. If a worker was working at the time of the survey, that is, an employment transition did not occur, that work spell is right censored. All work spells except the right-censored work spells end with the event of leaving the current workplace. There is no left-censoring in the event history data because it contains information on the complete retrospective work history of an individual.

Since the event history data are for investigating factors that have influenced employment stability for Korean employees, the analysis will be restricted to those who have ever been employed. The analysis will be further restricted to those who had completed their schooling process by the time of the survey; the records for 32 individuals in the original data, who were students at the time of the survey, were dropped. This is because the risk period in this study begins when a respondent finishes his or her full-time, formal education. If a respondent does not have any formal education, the risk period starts when he or she becomes 12 years old. The spells for compulsory military service and the work spells interrupted by compulsory military service will also be excluded from the analysis because they are irrelevant to the purposes of this study. After these restrictions, the number of individuals in the event history data is reduced to 2,397, and 3,505 work spells and 21,098 person-years or observations are analyzed.

As mentioned earlier in this chapter, the data for investigating factors that have influenced the desirability of transition outcomes will be created from the event history data. In other words, it will be created by keeping only the last person-years of the 2,375 work spells that are not right-censored in the event history data. The second data, therefore, include only 2,375 observations. As mentioned in Chapter 3, the observations in the second data will have five employment statuses—entrepreneurship, new employment in internal labor markets, self-employment, new employment in external labor markets, and nonemployment—as destinations of employment transitions, as defined in Chapter 3. These statuses will be operationalized later in this chapter.

Statistical Models

The method of analysis for the data containing all 21,098 person-years must be appropriate for time-varying, as well as time-constant, variables. Event history methods satisfy this requirement, and will be used in this study. The data containing only the last person-years of the 2,375 work spells that are not right-censored will be analyzed by ordered logit models, also known as proportional odds models.

Event history methods consist of discrete- and continuous-time models. Discrete-time models, rather than continuous-time models, are appropriate for the event history data in this study for the following reasons. First, the unit of employment duration in the event history data, a year, is coarse. Second, discrete-time models assume that we know only that an event occurred within a given interval. Specifically, discrete-time binomial logit models will be fit to the event history data.

In order to investigate factors that have influenced employment stability, overall employment transition rates need to be estimated using a main-effects binomial logit model and an interaction binomial logit model. Suppose that π_t is the conditional probability that an employee leaves a workplace in the current year t, given that he or she has not left the workplace yet. Then, a main-effects binomial logit model to be fit to the event history data is

$$\log[\pi_t/(1-\pi_t)] = \alpha + \beta^T X$$

where α is a baseline logit, β^T is a vector of coefficients to be estimated, and X is a vector of time-constant and time-varying covariates, which consist of individual-, structure-, and time-level independent variables.

An interaction binomial logit model assumes the same form, except that interaction terms between the variable for labor market structure and the other independent variables are also included in X. An assumption for this interaction model is that including such interaction terms should improve the fit of the main-effects binomial logit model.

In order to investigate whether or not there is any dependence of employment transition on employment duration, dummy variables for employment duration will be included in X in both the main-effects and the interaction models. If these dummy variables are included, α is a baseline logit at the reference time interval. Dummy variables for cohort will also be included in X in both models in order to control for cohort size effects.

In order to investigate factors that have influenced the desirability of transition outcomes, a main-effects ordered logit model and an interaction ordered logit model will be used. In Chapter 3, I argued that the desirability of transition outcomes among new employment statuses is in the following order from the least to the most desirable destination statuses: nonemployment ($j = 1$), new employment in external labor markets ($j = 2$), self-employment ($j = 3$), new employment in internal labor markets ($j = 4$), and entrepreneurship ($j = 5$). With π_j = the probability that an employee moves to state j, the ordered or cumulative probabilities that he or she moves to state j or below is

$$P(Y \le j) = \pi_1 + \ldots + \pi_j, j = 1, 2, 3, 4, 5.$$

Then, the ordered logits of the four ordered probabilities are

$$\text{logit}[P(Y \le j)] = \log[(\pi_1 + \ldots + \pi_j) / (\pi_{j+1} + \ldots + \pi_5)], \ j = 1, 2, 3, 4.$$

On the basis of these formulations, I form a main-effects ordered logit model

$$\text{logit}[P\,(Y \le j)] = \alpha_j - \beta^T X, \quad j = 1, 2, 3, 4$$

where α_j is a cut point parameter for j, which is nondecreasing in j, β^T is a vector of coefficients to be estimated, and X is a vector of covariates, which consist of individual-, structure-, and time-level independent variables.

An interaction ordered logit model assumes the same form, except that interaction terms between the variable for labor market structure and the other independent variables are also included in X. An assumption for this interaction model is that including such interaction terms should improve the fit of the main-effects ordered logit model.

A variable for employment duration will be included in X in both the main-effects and the interaction models in order to investigate the existence of any dependence of employment transition on employment duration. Dummy variables for cohort will also be included in X in both models in order to control for cohort size effects.

It needs to be noted that β^T does not have a j subscript, so it captures an identical effect of X on the log odds of moving to j state or below (Agresti 1996: 212). It also needs to be noted that if an estimated coefficient from β^T is positive, Y is more likely to fall at the high end of the scale as a covariate associated with that coefficient increases (Agresti 1996: 214).

Operationalizing Independent Variables

Table 4-1 shows how the independent variables in this study are defined. The independent variables are classified as individual-, structure-, and time-level variables, interaction terms between the variable for labor market structure and the rest of the three-level variables, and variables for cohort and employment duration.

Individual-Level Variables

Middle School, *High School*, and *College* are dummy variables for workers' completed formal education levels and represent workers' general human capital.[1]

In Chapter 3, I argued that various kinds of gender and gender-related restrictions decrease employment stability and the desirability of transition outcomes for Korean women. In order to incorporate these restrictions in the analysis at the same time, I classify Korean workers into (1) female workers with few childcare and housework responsibilities (*Female Without Young Children*), (2) male workers (*Male*), and (3) female workers with greater childcare and housework responsibilities (reference for *Female Without Young Children* and *Male*). In other words, *Female Without Young Children* and *Male* will be used to

Table 4-1. Definitions of Independent Variables

Independent Variable	Definition
Individual Level	
Education	
(Reference)	One has graduated from elementary school or has no formal education.
Middle School	1 if one has graduated from middle school, 0 otherwise.
High School	1 if one has graduated from high school, 0 otherwise.
College	1 if one has graduated from junior college or higher, 0 otherwise.
Gender and Gender-Related Factors	
(Reference)	Female and either (1) married and before the first child-birth or (2) the last child is less than 7 years old, 0 otherwise.
Female Without Young Children	1 if female and either (1) unmarried and childless or (2) the last child is more than 6 years old.
Male	1 if male, 0 otherwise.
Structure Level	
ILM (Internal Labor Market)	1 if one is in an internal labor market, 0 otherwise. One has been in an internal labor market in either of the following two cases. First, one's organization has externally hired people with a similar rank to one's final rank, which is not that of a top-level manager, and people of a similar rank to one's final rank have a possibility of promotion. Second, one's organization has internally hired people with a similar rank to one's final rank. In other words, one has been in an internal labor market if in the questionnaire presented in Appendix A, (1) one chooses 0, 1, or 2 for c141-c149, 2 for c151-c159, and 3 or 4 for c161-c169 or (2) one chooses 0, 1, 2, or 3 for c141-c149 and 1 for c151-c159.
Large Organization	1 if one's organization hires 500 employees or more or one works in a public organization, 0 otherwise.
Unionized Organization	1 if there has been a labor union in one's organization while one is employed, 0 otherwise.

explore whether or not gender and gender-related factors such as childcare and housework have affected employment transition patterns in Korea over time.

Table 4-1. Definitions of Independent Variables (*Continued*)

Independent Variable	Definition
Time	
(Reference)	One works in 1987–1996.
Before 1961	1 if one works before 1961, 0 otherwise.
1961 Through 1986	1 if one works in 1961–1986, 0 otherwise.
Interaction Terms	First-order interactions between *ILM* and each of *Middle School* through *1961 Through 1986*.
Cohort	
(Reference)	Born in 1961 or later.
Cohort 1930s	1 if born in 1940 or earlier, 0 otherwise.
Cohort 1940s	1 if born in 1941–1950, 0 otherwise.
Cohort 1950s	1 if born in 1951–1960, 0 otherwise.
Year n	(For the binomial logit models only) 1 if the *n*th year of a work spell (*n* is greater than 1 and *n* = 15 represents 15 or greater), 0 otherwise (Reference: the first year of a work spell).
Work Years	(For the ordered logit models only) Number of years of working at the current workplace continuously.

I also argued in Chapter 3 that employers prefer (1) male workers to female workers, and (2) workers with few childcare and housework responsibilities to workers with greater childcare and housework responsibilities. This suggests that the desirability of the above three types of workers for employers is in the following order from the least to the most desirable types: (1) female workers with greater childcare and housework responsibilities, (2) female workers with few childcare and housework responsibilities, and (3) male workers.

Structure-Level Variables

In this study, the structure-level independent variables refer to labor market structure and such organization-level characteristics as organizational size and unionism.

ILM will be used to distinguish between internal labor markets and external labor markets in which workers are employed. As discussed in Chapter 3, we need to identify (1) a job ladder, and (2) either entry port only at the bottom or internal promotions on that job ladder in order to define a labor market as an internal labor market.

Information on whether a labor market has a job ladder, however, is not available in the data. In this study, I identify internal promotions with a job ladder. That is to say, if internal promotions occur in a labor market, that labor market is regarded as having a job ladder. The identification of internal promotions with a job ladder is indirectly supported by some information in the data. The data contain two questions related to the existence of a job ladder at the current or most recent workplace as of the time of the survey: one about formal training and the other about job transfer through a job rotation system (Questions d10 and d11 in Appendix A). I suggest that if an organization provides its workers with formal training or job transfer, it has a hierarchy of jobs requiring different levels of skills and knowledge, which was defined as a job ladder in Chapter 3. The data also contain a question about how many times a respondent has been promoted at the current or most recent workplace (Question d14 in Appendix A). It turns out that the majority (75.2 percent) of workers who have been promoted at their current or most recent workplaces have received formal training or have experienced job transfer.

The criteria of entry port only at the bottom and internal promotions are used to define an internal labor market in Table 4-1. The first case for an internal labor market suggested in Table 4-1 is for workers at entry port at the bottom. In other words, if an organization hires all workers at a particular rank from outside and provides them with a possibility of promotion, that organization is regarded as having an internal labor market. It is not clear from the data, however, whether or not one or more ranks above that particular rank are also filled by external recruitments. Yet, if that particular rank filled entirely by external recruitments provides its occupants with a possibility of promotion, it is likely that at least the rank right above that particular rank is filled by internal promotions. One caveat is that the rank of a top-level manager cannot be entry port of an internal labor market because it cannot provide a top-level manager with further promotion opportunities. The second case for an internal labor market suggested in Table 4-1 is for workers above entry port at the bottom. If an organization hires all workers at a particular rank from inside, that organization is regarded as having an internal labor market.

As seen in Table 4-1 and Appendix A, *ILM* is generated from information on the entire period during which one is employed in an organization (Questions c151-c159 in Appendix A), and from information on the time when one leaves the organization (Questions c141-c149 and c161-c169 in Appendix A). *ILM*, therefore, is not completely time-varying, for the observation unit of the data for investigating factors that have influenced employment stability is a person-year. This limitation of *ILM* requires an assumption that labor market structure does not change while a worker stays in the same labor market. The problem this assumption raises can be lessened to some degree if the labor market structure of an organization is stable for at least several years. Because the mean duration of all work spells is 6.14 years, as shown in Table 4-4, and 58.36 percent of employees have more than 3 years of employment duration in the data, I suggest that the problem the above assumption might cause may be minute in this case.

Large Organization and *Unionized Organization* are organization-level variables. They have similar problems to those of *ILM* since they are not completely time-varying either. I argue, however, that small- to medium-sized firms rarely become large firms and vice versa because the threshold for a large firm is defined as 500 or more employees, which is fairly high. *Unionized Organization* is more problematic since unions can be established or disorganized at a certain point in time while a worker is employed in an organization. *Unionized Organization*, therefore, should be interpreted as a variable indicating whether a union ever existed while a worker was employed in an organization.

Time-Level Variables

Before 1961 and *1961 Through 1986* are defined based on changes in the Korean state's economic development strategies and labor market policies as suggested in Chapter 2. (1) From 1953 to 1960, i.e., during the slow economic recovery from the aftermath of the Korean War in 1950-1953, the Korean state hardly implemented any systematic economic development strategies and labor market policies (*Before 1961*). (2) As of 1961, the state embarked on export-oriented industrialization and began to strengthen labor controls, and as of 1973, it launched a vigorous drive for heavy-industrialization and began to strengthen labor controls even more (*1961 Through 1986*). (3) Since 1987, the state had to relax its harsh labor control policies to some degree in the face of political democratization caused by strong political challenges from workers and students (reference for *Before 1961* and *1961 Through 1986*).

Interaction Terms

Terms for the first-order interactions between *ILM* and each of the above individual- and organization-level variables will be included in the interaction models for the binomial and ordered logistic regressions in order to explore whether or not *ILM* has different effects on employment transition patterns in Korea by each of the individual- and organization-level variables. These interaction terms will be analyzed since the main focus of this study is placed on the various ways in which labor market structure affects employment transition patterns in Korea.

Terms for the first-order interactions between *ILM* and each of the variables for time, *Before 1961* and *1961 Through 1986*, in Table 4-1 will be included in the interaction models for the binomial and ordered logistic regressions in order to investigate whether or not the degree to which labor market structure affects employment transition patterns has changed in Korea over time.

Variables for Cohort and Employment Duration

Dummy variables, *Cohort 1930s*, *Cohort 1940s*, and *Cohort 1950s*, will be included in the analysis to investigate if there are cohort size effects on employment transition patterns. In general, cohort size effects can be defined as the effects of the size of a particular birth cohort on the characteristics of that birth cohort. For example, large birth cohorts are more likely to be in a difficult labor market position constantly than small ones (Oppenheimer 1982: 42). Considering the fact that Korea's population has significantly increased for the last four decades, I suggest that cohort size effects may be substantial in Korea. For these reasons, cohort size effects will be controlled when the effects of other factors on employment transition patterns are investigated.

Dummy variables, *Year 2* through *Year 15*, will be included in the binomial logit model investigating factors that have influenced employment stability in order to investigate whether or not there is any dependence of employment transition on employment duration in Korea. As a control variable, *Work Years* will be included in the ordered logit model investigating factors that have influenced the desirability of transition outcomes.

Operationalizing Destinations of Employment Transitions

In the Statistical Models section of this chapter, I showed that the dependent variable for the ordered logit model is logit$[P\ (Y \leq j)]$ where $P\ (Y \leq j)$ is the ordered probabilities that a worker moves to state j or below and j is nonemployment, new employment in external labor markets, self-employment, or new employment in internal labor markets. Table 4-2 shows the definitions of these four destination statuses of employment transitions along with the destination status of entrepreneurship.

Predicted Effects

Based on the definitions of the independent variables and the five destination statuses of employment transitions so far, the predicted effects of the independent variables on employment transition patterns are summarized in Tables 4-3 using expected signs of the coefficients of the independent variables.

Table 4-2. Definitions of Destination Statuses of Employment Transitions for
         Ordered Logit Models

Destination Status	Definition
Entrepreneurship	The status of not being paid by anyone else for one's work and of hiring five or more employees.
Employment in ILMs	Employment in internal labor markets ($ILM = 1$ as defined in Table 4-1).
Self-Employment	The status of not being paid by anyone else for one's work and of hiring less than five employees.
Employment in ELMs	Employment in external labor markets ($ILM = 0$ as defined in Table 4-1).
Nonemployment	The status in which one is not in any one of the above statuses, i.e., the status in which the gap between any two statuses above is more than one year.

A main-effects model and an interaction model will be fit to both the data on employment stability and the data on the desirability of transition outcomes, so that Table 4-3 combines two sets of expected results, i.e., expected results from the main-effects models and expected results from the interaction models. Therefore, the effects of the noninteraction variables refer to the effects in the main-effects models, and those of the interaction terms refer to the effects in the interaction models.

Descriptive Statistics

Table 4-4 presents the descriptive statistics for the most important characteristics of the sample. All statistics in Table 4-4 are weighted by the weighting variable that makes the sample nationally representative.

Some descriptive statistics in Table 4-4 are worth mentioning. First, the majority of respondents are relatively young: The mean age is 37.98, the modal age category is 31-40, and the modal cohort category is the cohort born in the 1960s or later. Second, 62.07 percent of respondents have middle or high school education, and 28.97 percent have more than high school education. These figures are fairly high considering the fact that Korea has been a developing country. The high proportion of Korean people with secondary and postsecondary education is a result of the fairly consistent and extensive investments in formal education by the Korean government as a strategy of meeting the large and increasing demand for skilled labor caused by Korea's rapid economic development.

Table 4-3. Predicted Effects of Independent Variables

Independent Variable	Probability of Leaving Current Workplace (Binomial Logit Models)	Probability of Having More Desirable Transition Outcomes* (Ordered Logit Models)
Individual Level		
Education (Reference: Elementary School or No Education)		
Middle School	–	+
High School	–	+
College	–	+
Gender and Gender-Related Factors (Reference: Female With Young Children)		
Female Without Young Children	–	+
Male	–	+
Structure Level		
ILM (Internal Labor Market)	–	+
Large Organization	–	+
Unionized Organization	–	+
Time (Reference: 1987 Through 1996)		
Before 1961	+	–
1961 Through 1986	+	–
Interaction Terms (In Interaction Models)		
Middle School×ILM	–	+
High School×ILM	–	+
College×ILM	–	+
Female Without Young Children×ILM	+	–
Male×ILM	–	+
Large Organization×ILM	–	+
Unionized Organization×ILM	–	+
Before 1961×ILM	+	–
1961 Through 1986×ILM	+	–

* Desirability of transition outcomes: entrepreneurship > employment in ILMs > self-employment > employment in ELMs > nonemployment.

Chapter 4

Table 4-4. Descriptive Statistics

Characteristic	Percent
Individual Level	
Age in 1996	
25-30	25.09
31-40	41.90
41-50	20.10
51-60	12.91
Age in 1996 (Continuous)	(Mean: 37.98 / S.D.: 9.34)
Completed Education	
Elementary School or No Education	8.95
Middle School	13.25
High School	48.82
Junior College or Higher	28.97
Gender	
Male	56.07
Female	43.93
Childcare and Housework Responsibility (Person-Year, Female)	
Few (*Female Without Young Children*)	79.18
Greater (Reference for *Female Without Young Children* and *Male*)	20.82
***N*th Year at a Workplace** (Person-Year)	
1	16.30
2	14.69
3	12.06
4	9.51
5	7.71
6	6.23
7-42	33.5
Work Years (Length of a Work Spell)	(Mean: 6.14 / S.D.: 5.72)
Cohort	
Born in the 1930s	6.21
Born in the 1940s	14.75
Born in the 1950s	31.28
Born in the 1960s or Later	47.76

Table 4-4. Descriptive Statistics (*Continued*)

Characteristic	Percent
Structure Level (Work Spell)	
Labor Market Structure	
Internal Labor Market	34.81
External Labor Market	65.19
Number of Employees	
500 or More or Public Organizations	18.08
Less Than 500	81.92
Existence of Labor Union	
Yes	24.28
No	75.72
Time (Person-Year)	
Before 1961	1.10
1961-1986	46.86
1987-1996	52.04

Note: All statistics are weighted by the weighting variable.

Table 4-5 shows the proportion of employment transition types by gender from the data including not only the spells for employees but also the spells for nonemployees, i.e., entrepreneurs and the self-employed. All percentages in Table 4-5 are weighted by the weighting variable as the statistics in Table 4-4.

Several characteristics in Table 4-5 can be pointed out. First, I note some characteristics that are related to the desirability of transition outcomes for workers in internal labor markets and workers in external labor markets. (1) For both men and women, both workers in internal labor markets and workers in external labor markets are more likely to move to the same employment status than to other employment statuses once they leave their current workplaces. This means that workers in internal labor markets show better transition outcomes than workers in external labor markets. (2) Male workers in internal labor markets are less likely to move to self-employment and nonemployment than male workers in external labor markets. This means that male workers in internal labor markets show better transition outcomes than male workers in external labor markets.

Second, entrepreneurship is the most difficult status to enter after a nonentrepreneur leaves his or her current status. Employment in an internal labor market is also fairly difficult to enter after a working person who is not employed in an internal labor market leaves his or her current status. These facts are consistent

Table 4-5. Proportion of Employment Transition Types by Gender (%)

Start of Spell \ End of Spell	Entrepreneurship	Employment in ILMs	Self-Employment	Employment in ELMs	Nonemployment	Total
Men						
Entrepreneurship	69.27 (12.72)	4.10	15.03	9.35	2.24	100.00 (n = 127)
Employment in ILMs	2.30	75.76 (21.56)	9.95	8.02	3.98	100.00 (n = 738)
Self-Employment	1.28	6.25	79.45 (18.29)	9.29	3.74	100.00 (n = 889)
Employment in ELMs	2.29	5.70	15.57	68.83 (30.23)	7.60	100.00 (n = 1,223)
Nonemployment	2.17	23.30	20.07	46.85	7.61 (0.00)	100.00 (n = 556)
Women						
Entrepreneurship	33.80 (17.26)	0.00	7.47	12.42	46.30	100.00 (n = 18)
Employment in ILMs	0.00	53.47 (24.32)	4.95	7.65	33.93	100.00 (n = 455)
Self-Employment	0.09	2.57	63.52 (21.61)	12.34	21.48	100.00 (n = 541)
Employment in ELMs	0.34	2.54	4.29	62.13 (36.23)	30.70	100.00 (n = 1,245)
Nonemployment	0.59	12.82	11.80	36.11	38.67 (0.00)	100.00 (n = 1,274)

Note: Unit is a spell. Values enclosed in parentheses in diagonal cells are from uncensored spells only, and values not enclosed in parentheses in diagonal cells are from all spells including censored spells as well. Spells for entrepreneurship, self-employment, and nonemployment are not used in the binomial and ordered logit models. All percentages are weighted by the weighting variable.

with the arguments presented in Chapter 3: Entrepreneurship is regarded as the most desirable new destination status because it provides chances of the greatest economic success and the highest autonomy in work. Employment in internal labor markets is more desirable than self-employment and employment in external labor markets because it provides higher earnings and better working conditions. The desirability of entrepreneurship and employment in internal labor markets, therefore, makes entrance into these two new statuses rather difficult.

Third, for both men and women, people in nonemployment are more likely to move to employment in external labor markets than to any other status except nonemployment. This is evidence that employment in external labor markets is less desirable than any other status except nonemployment, for people in non-employment can be regarded as being in the least favorable position when searching for new workplaces. On the other hand, for both men and women, people in nonemployment are less likely to move to entrepreneurship than to any other employment status. This is evidence that entrepreneurship is more desirable than any other employment status for the reason mentioned above.

Fourth, for both men and women, employees tend to become employees again, and nonemployees, who consist of entrepreneurs and the self-employed, tend to become nonemployees again once they leave their workplaces. This suggests that the whole employment sector is separated to some degree from the sector for entrepreneurship and self-employment in terms of employment transitions. If we look at the rows for both men and women in which the start of a spell is nonemployment, we notice that people in nonemployment are more likely to enter employment in internal labor markets and employment in external labor markets than entrepreneurship and self-employment. This implies that nonemployment plays a role of separating employees from nonemployees to a certain degree in terms of employment transitions.

Fifth, if we look at the diagonal cells for both men and women, especially for women, we notice that the majority of the spells except the nonemployment spells are censored or followed by the spells of the same status. This means that (1) employment transitions have not occurred yet for a significant proportion of respondents by the time of the survey, and (2) a significant proportion of employment transitions have occurred between the same employment statuses.

Sixth, for all types of working people, especially for entrepreneurs and workers in internal labor markets, women are more likely to move to nonemployment than men. This is strong evidence that employment stability and the desirability of transition outcomes are significantly lower for women than for men.

Although Table 4-5 shows employment transition patterns in the Korean labor market to a certain degree, it is stratified only by gender and therefore does not reveal other important characteristics of employment transition patterns. In order to grasp important characteristics of employment transition patterns in Korea that are influenced by factors other than gender, multivariate analyses are needed, as demonstrated in Chapters 5 and 6.

Notes

1 It is desirable to include variables for workers' firm-specific human capital, too. The data, however, do not provide any information on workers' firm-specific human capital. Therefore, firm-specific human capital will not be used in this study.

5 Employment Stability

As suggested in Chapter 1, employment stability is the first aspect of employment transitions related to workers' economic and social well-being in Korea. In this chapter, detailed working hypotheses on factors affecting employment stability in Korea will be presented, followed by discussions on whether or not results of the analysis support the working hypotheses, comparisons between results of this study and results from previous research, and a discussion of the implications of these comparisons for factors affecting employment stability in countries other than Korea.

Working Hypotheses

The working hypotheses for both the main-effects binomial logit model and the interaction binomial logit model are presented in Table 5-1. They are based on definitions of the independent variables in Table 4-1 and on the predicted effects of the independent variables on employment stability shown in Table 4-3. The rightmost column in Table 5-1 shows (1) whether or not each working hypothesis is supported by the result of the analysis in Table 5-2, and (2) if it is supported, whether it is supported partially, marginally, or strongly.

Results of Analysis

Results of the analysis of factors affecting employment stability in Korea are shown in Table 5-2. These include results from both the main-effects binomial logit model and the interaction binomial logit model.

A likelihood ratio test comparing fitted values from the main-effects model and the interaction model produces a chi-square statistic of 14.89 with 9 degrees of freedom and a significance level of 0.094. This result means that the interaction terms are jointly significant at the 0.094 level. Therefore, it is hard to say that the interaction model improves the fit of the main-effects model.

Comparisons between signs of the coefficients in Table 5-2 and signs of the predicted effects of the independent variables on the probability of leaving the current workplace shown in Table 4-3 are presented in Table 5-3.

Table 5-1. Working Hypotheses: Binomial Logit Models

Independent Variable	Working Hypothesis	Support From Result
Individual Level		
Education	• Workers with higher level of completed education are less likely to leave their workplaces than workers with lower level of completed education.	Partial
	• The above tendency is stronger in internal labor markets (ILMs) than in external labor markets (ELMs).	No
Gender and Gender-Related Factors	• Female workers with few childcare and housework responsibilities (i.e., female workers who are unmarried and childless or whose youngest children are over 6 years of age) are less likely to leave their workplaces than female workers with greater childcare and housework responsibilities (i.e., female workers who are married and before their first childbirths or whose youngest children are under 7 years of age).	Strong
	• The above tendency is stronger in ILMs than in ELMs.	No
	• Male workers are less likely to leave their workplaces than female workers with greater childcare and housework responsibilities.	Strong
	• The above tendency is stronger in ILMs than in ELMs.	No
Structure Level		
Labor Market Structure	• Workers in ILMs are less likely to leave their workplaces than workers in ELMs.	Strong
Organizational Size	• Workers in private organizations hiring more than 499 employees or in public organizations are less likely to leave their workplaces than workers in private organizations hiring less than 500 employees.	Marginal
	• The above tendency is stronger in ILMs than in ELMs.	Strong
Unionism	• Workers in unionized organizations are less likely to leave their workplaces than workers in nonunionized organizations.	Strong
	• The above tendency is stronger in ILMs than in ELMs.	No

Table 5-1. Working Hypotheses: Binomial Logit Models (*Continued*)

Independent Variable	Working Hypothesis	Support From Result
Time	• Workers were more likely to leave their workplaces before 1961 than in 1987-1996.	Marginal
	• The degree to which workers in ILMs are less likely to leave their workplaces than workers in ELMs was lower before 1961 than in 1987-1996.	No
	• Workers were more likely to leave their workplaces in 1961-1986 than in 1987-1996.	Strong
	• The degree to which workers in ILMs are less likely to leave their workplaces than workers in ELMs was lower in 1961-1986 than in 1987-1996.	No

Labor Market Structure

The estimated coefficient for *ILM* shows that workers in internal labor markets are exp(-0.395) = 0.674 times as likely to leave their workplaces as workers in external labor markets. Employers in internal labor markets try to reduce employment transitions in order to make job ladders operate more efficiently, so they provide workers in higher positions on job ladders with higher wages and better working conditions. Additionally, employees in internal labor markets try to stay at their current workplaces as long as possible in order to take advantage of promotion opportunities job ladders provide. Employment stability, therefore, is higher in internal labor markets than in external labor markets.

This result is consistent with results of the studies discussed in Chapter 3, which show the effects of labor market structure on employment stability in the United States (Petersen and Spilerman 1990) and in Korea (Yoo 1996). The fact that internal labor market structure increases employment stability in a developing country such as Korea as well as in an advanced industrial country like the United States implies the possibility that the influence of labor market structure on employment stability emerges once a country's industrialization reaches a moderate level. This possibility coincides with the assumption underlying the definition of an internal labor market used in this study. In other words, an important precondition for the characteristics of an internal labor market, i.e., a job ladder with entry port only at the bottom or with movement up this ladder, is that a country should already have achieved at least a moderate degree of industrial development.

Table 5-2. Results: Binomial Logit Models

Independent Variable	Main-Effects Model		Interaction Model	
	Coeffi-cient	Robust S.E.	Coeffi-cient	Robust S.E.
Individual Level				
Education (Reference: Elementary School or No Education)				
Middle School	-0.151	0.167	-0.164	0.190
High School	-0.084	0.159	-0.027	0.183
College	-0.437**	0.171	-0.414*	0.201
Gender and Gender-Related Factors (Reference: Female With Young Children)				
Female Without Young Children	-1.311***	0.104	-1.298***	0.128
Male	-1.490***	0.099	-1.503***	0.124
Structure Level				
ILM (Internal Labor Market)	-0.395***	0.062	-0.056	0.393
Large Organization	-0.137†	0.075	0.007	0.099
Unionized Organization	-0.281***	0.066	-0.393***	0.085
Time (Reference: 1987 Through 1996)				
Before 1961	0.580†	0.328	0.900*	0.364
1961 Through 1986	0.149*	0.066	0.147*	0.075
Interaction Terms				
Middle School×ILM			-0.115	0.367
High School×ILM			-0.412	0.347
College×ILM			-0.312	0.365
Female Without Young Children×ILM			-0.071	0.220
Male×ILM			0.025	0.204
Large Organization×ILM			-0.347*	0.156
Unionized Organization×ILM			0.280*	0.138
Before 1961×ILM			-0.721	0.595
1961 Through 1986×ILM			-0.002	0.123

Table 5-2. Results: Binomial Logit Models (*Continued*)

Independent Variable	Main-Effects Model		Interaction Model	
	Coeffi-cient	Robust S.E.	Coeffi-cient	Robust S.E.
Cohort (Reference: Born in 1961 or Later)				
Cohort 1930s	-0.747***	0.130	-0.753***	0.132
Cohort 1940s	-0.803***	0.097	-0.783***	0.098
Cohort 1950s	-0.560***	0.075	-0.555***	0.075
Year n (Reference: First Year)				
Year 2	0.802***	0.097	0.804***	0.097
Year 3	0.983***	0.100	0.986***	0.100
Year 4	0.749***	0.109	0.751***	0.109
Year 5	0.922***	0.113	0.929***	0.113
Year 6	0.897***	0.120	0.903***	0.121
Year 7	0.706***	0.130	0.711***	0.131
Year 8	0.739***	0.141	0.745***	0.141
Year 9	0.509**	0.168	0.514**	0.168
Year 10	0.470**	0.182	0.477**	0.182
Year 11	-0.078	0.251	-0.070	0.251
Year 12	0.123	0.240	0.130	0.239
Year 13	0.351	0.247	0.359	0.246
Year 14	0.282	0.264	0.287	0.264
Year 15 through *Year 42*	0.429**	0.148	0.437**	0.148
Constant	-0.794***	0.198	-0.832***	0.227
Log-Likelihood	-6,157.993		-6,150.550	
Degrees of Freedom	20,289		20,280	
Number of Observations	20,317		20,317	

†$p < .1$, *$p < .05$, **$p < .01$, ***$p < .001$ (two-tailed tests).

The effect of labor market structure on employment stability in developing countries other than Korea can be predicted based on the above discussion. Internal labor market structure increases employment stability in those developing countries that have already achieved at least a moderate degree of industrial development.

Table 5-3. Comparisons Between Predicted and Estimated Effects of
Independent Variables on Employment Stability: Binomial Logit
Models

Independent Variable	Predicted Effect From Hypothesis	Estimated Effect From Analysis
Individual Level		
Education (Reference: Elementary School or No Education)		
Middle School	−	
High School	−	
College	−	−
Gender and Gender-Related Factors (Reference: Female With Young Children)		
Female Without Young Children	−	−
Male	−	−
Structure Level		
ILM (Internal Labor Market)	−	−
Large Organization	−	−
Unionized Organization	−	−
Time (Reference: 1987 Through 1996)		
Before 1961	+	+
1961 Through 1986	+	+
Interaction Terms (In Interaction Models)		
Middle School×ILM	−	
High School×ILM	−	
College×ILM	−	
Male×ILM	−	
Female Without Young Children×ILM	−	
Large Organization×ILM	−	−
Unionized Organization×ILM	−	+
Before 1961×ILM	+	
1961 Through 1986×ILM	+	

Human Capital

The estimated coefficient for *College* shows that workers with more than high school education are exp(-0.437) = 0.646 times as likely to leave their workplaces as workers with less than middle school education. The skill level of jobs for workers with more than high school education is higher than that for workers with less than middle school education in Korea. The expected gains from a job match rise with increases in the skill level of a job. Workers with more than high school education, therefore, are more committed to staying at their current workplaces in order to realize their expected gains, i.e., in order to increase their wages and improve their working conditions.

The fact that the estimated coefficient for *College* is negative and significant may imply that the greater amount of general human capital has increased employment stability in Korea over time. However, the estimated coefficients for *Middle School* and *High School* in Table 5-2, which are not statistically significant, do not support this implication. In other words, they show that workers with middle school education and workers with high school education are statistically as likely to leave their workplaces as workers with less than middle school education.

In Korea, there is virtually no significant difference between the amount of general human capital acquired by workers with middle or high school education and the amount of general human capital acquired by workers with less than middle school education. This makes the difference in the job skill level between the two types of workers virtually insignificant. As mentioned earlier, the expected gains from a job match rise with increases in the skill level of a job. Therefore, workers with middle or high school education are not more committed to staying at their current workplaces to increase their wages and improve their working conditions than workers with less than middle school education.

Another possible explanation may be that there are no significant advantages for workers with middle or high school education over workers with less than middle school education in terms of wages and working conditions despite the higher labor productivity of the former. If this is the case, we can say that there is a tendency for job rewards, which affect employment stability, to be leveled off among workers with less than college education in the Korean labor market.

Although the estimated coefficient for *College* is statistically significant, the estimated coefficient for the term of the interaction between *College* and *ILM* is not statistically significant. The mechanism for this result is that generally in Korea, the degree to which the tasks of higher positions on a job ladder are more complex and firm-specific is not enough for higher positions on a job ladder to be filled significantly more often by workers with more than high school education than by workers with less than middle school education.

This result, that more general human capital partially increases employment stability in Korea, coincides to a certain degree with the result of a study mentioned in Chapter 3 that more general human capital is associated with higher employment stability in the United States (Mincer 1962). This may be because the effective formal education system enables higher formal education to produce actually more general human capital both in Korea and in an advanced industrial country such as the United States.

Furthermore, I suggest that the effect of general human capital on employment stability in developing countries other than Korea also depends on the effectiveness of the formal education system of those countries. In other words, I expect that more general human capital increases employment stability in developing countries other than Korea if higher formal education actually produces more general human capital in those countries as well.

Gender

The estimated coefficient for *Female Without Young Children* shows that female workers with few childcare and housework responsibilities are exp(-1.311) = 0.270 times as likely to leave their workplaces as female workers with greater childcare and housework responsibilities. The estimated coefficient for *Male* shows that male workers are exp(-1.490) = 0.225 times as likely to leave their workplaces as female workers with greater childcare and housework responsibilities.

Employers prefer female workers with few childcare and housework responsibilities and male workers to female workers with greater childcare and housework responsibilities because they believe that the former have higher labor productivity and contribute more to increased profits than the latter. Female workers with few childcare and housework responsibilities and male workers know this, so that they are more committed to staying at their current workplaces in order to increase their wages and improve their working conditions.

I suggested in the *Individual-Level Variables* subsection of Chapter 4 that for employers, (1) female workers with greater childcare and housework responsibilities are the least desirable, (2) male workers are the most desirable, and (3) female workers with few childcare and housework responsibilities are in between. If this suggestion is correct, the absolute value of the coefficient for *Male* should be significantly greater than that for *Female Without Young Children*. A statistical test confirms this: The chi-square statistic with 1 degree of freedom for the null hypothesis that the coefficient for *Female Without Young Children* is the same as the coefficient for *Male* is 7.56. The significance level for the test is 0.006. Therefore, I reject the null hypothesis with considerable confidence and conclude that *Male* has a greater influence on the log odds of leaving the current workplace than *Female Without Young Children*.

In Chapter 3, I argued that internal labor market structure allows female workers with few childcare and housework responsibilities and male workers to have advantages over female workers with greater childcare and housework responsibilities in terms of employment stability due to the beliefs of both employers and workers: (1) the employers' belief that the former contribute more to the efficient operation of job ladders, and (2) the workers' belief that the former have more chance of promotion on job ladders. The fact that the estimated effects of these interactions are not significant suggests that these beliefs are not so strong as to allow the former to have even higher employment stability in internal labor markets.

One reason why labor market structure has not significantly changed the influences of gender and gender-related factors on employment stability in Korea over time as shown in Table 5-2 may be that the influences of gender and gender-related factors on employment stability have been so strong that labor market structure has had little room to change them. This reasoning may be supported by the fact that the effects of *Female Without Young Children* and *Male* on employment stability are strongly negative and highly significant as mentioned above.

The finding that men and less responsibilities of childcare and housework increase employment stability in Korea is consistent with results of studies mentioned in Chapter 3 showing the influences of marriage, childbirth, childcare, and household responsibilities on employment stability for women in advanced industrial countries such as the United States and Japan, as well as in several developing countries including Korea. This consistency implies that institutional and cultural practices based on patriarchal values, which cause less stable employment for female workers, persist across many countries although their strength may vary.

Organization-Level Characteristics

The estimated coefficient for *Large Organization* shows that workers in large private organizations or in public organizations are exp(-0.137) = 0.872 times as likely to leave their workplaces as workers in small private organizations. Three factors contribute to this result. First, the cost of recruiting and training workers is higher in large organizations because large organizations use more complicated technologies. Second, large organizations are able to provide workers with higher wages and better working conditions because they have greater resources based on greater market power. Third, working conditions are better in large organizations because more complicated technologies used in large organizations lead to the adoption of personnel management based on administrative rules and procedures rather than on arbitrary decisions of supervisors.

The estimated coefficient for *Unionized Organization* shows that workers in unionized organizations are exp(-0.281) = 0.755 times as likely to leave their workplaces as workers in nonunionized organizations. This result is due to two factors. First, labor unions' bargaining power causes the union wage effect. Second, easier communication between workers and management in unionized organizations makes it easier for less desirable working conditions to be changed.

The hypothesized effect of an interaction between organizational size and labor market structure is marginally supported by the result in Table 5-2. This result is explained by the following mechanism. Most positions on job ladders require different levels and kinds of skills and knowledge of workers, and job ladders' greater efficiency helps make more profits. Job ladders in internal labor markets, therefore, make more complicated technologies used in large organizations even more complicated and the greater market power of large organizations even greater.

The hypothesized effect of an interaction between unionism and labor market structure is not supported by this analysis. In fact, the direction of the estimated effect of the interaction is opposite to that predicted in the hypothesis: Table 5-2 shows that the estimated effect of the interaction is *positive* and significant. This implies that in Korea over time, the degree to which unionism increases employment stability has been higher in *external* labor markets than in internal labor markets.

In Chapter 3, I suggested that the degree to which unionism increases employment stability is higher in internal labor markets than in external labor markets because job ladders in internal labor markets make the greater bargaining power of workers in unionized organizations even greater, and make easier communication between workers and management in unionized organizations even easier. The contradicting result in Table 5-2 implies that in Korea over time, the structure of *external* labor markets has made the greater bargaining power of workers in unionized organizations even greater, and has made easier communication between workers and management in unionized organizations even easier. In other words, it implies that the degree to which labor unions have greater bargaining power and make communication between workers and management easier has been higher in external labor markets than in internal labor markets in Korea over time.

This finding may be justified by a special characteristic of labor unions in Korea over time. As mentioned in Chapter 2, Korean workers have faced strict labor controls by the state. In order to protect and promote economic and political interests, workers in external labor markets, who have hardly had any means to do so, have had to rely on labor unions more than workers in internal labor markets, who have had more means to do so by virtue of their more favorable positions in the labor market. Labor unions in external labor markets, therefore, have been more active in increasing their bargaining power and improving communication between workers and management by increasing the solidarity of their members. As a result, the degree to which unionism increases employment stability has been higher in external labor markets than in internal labor markets in Korea over time.

It needs to be noted that the direction in which labor market structure changes the influence of organizational size on employment stability is directly opposite to the direction in which it changes the influence of unionism on employment stability. This may imply that organizational size and unionism are significantly different organization-level characteristics affecting employment stability in Korea.

As mentioned above, the influence of organizational size on employment stability can be specified as the influence of three factors: (1) the amount of the cost of recruiting and training workers, which is affected by the complexity of technologies used in an organization, (2) the level of wages, which is affected by the degree of the market share of an organization, and (3) the desirability of working conditions, which is affected by the degree of the market share of an organization and by the complexity of technologies used in an organization via the characteristic of personnel management. Since these factors can largely be regarded as economic factors, we can say that organizational size represents an economic aspect of organizations' influences on employment stability.

As also mentioned above, the influence of unionism on employment stability can be specified as the influence of two factors: (1) the union wage effect based on labor unions' bargaining power, and (2) the easier changes of less desirable working conditions based on ease of communication between workers and management. These two factors, in turn, are based on the solidarity of union members. The solidarity of union members is basically a matter of how well a labor union organizes and mobilizes its members and resources in order to accomplish its goals. In this sense, unionism represents a political aspect of organizations' influences on employment stability.

The estimated effect of an interaction between labor market structure and organizational size shows that labor market structure operates to intensify the effect of an economic factor, organizational size, on employment stability in Korea. The direction of the effect of labor market structure on employment stability, however, is reversed by a political factor in Korea, unionism. A special characteristic of Korean development mentioned above provides a background for this reversal. Strict labor controls by the state, which can be regarded as another political factor, have unintentionally spurred labor unions in external labor markets to make more intensive efforts to overcome such controls.

These findings coincide with results of the studies mentioned in Chapter 3 investigating the influences of organizational size and unionism on employment stability. First, the fact that larger organizational size increases employment stability in Korea is consistent with the fact that larger organizational size increases employment stability in West Germany (Carroll and Mayer 1986) and in the United States (Rebitzer 1986). This consistency implies that a moderate degree of industrialization, among other things, brings large organizations more complex technologies and higher market shares in a developing country such as

Korea, as well as in advanced industrial countries as such West Germany and the United States.

Furthermore, I suggest that the effect of organizational size on employment stability in developing countries other than Korea also depends on the degree of industrialization in those countries. In other words, I expect that larger organizational size increases employment stability in other developing countries if those developing countries have also achieved at least a moderate degree of industrialization.

Second, the fact that unionism increases employment stability in Korea is consistent with the fact that unionism increases employment stability in the United States (Blau and Kahn 1983). From this similarity, I infer that the solidarity of union members based on fairly active labor movements leads to the union wage effect via labor unions' bargaining power, and to easier communication between workers and management both in Korea and in advanced industrial countries like the United States.

Moreover, I suggest that the effect of unionism on employment stability in developing countries other than Korea also depends on the degree of labor movement activity in those countries. I expect that unionism increases employment stability in developing countries if fairly active labor movements exist in those countries as well.

Time

The estimated coefficient for *Before 1961* shows that workers employed before 1961 were $\exp(0.580) = 1.786$ times as likely to leave their workplaces as workers employed in 1987-1996. The estimated coefficient for *1961 Through 1986* shows that workers employed in 1961-1986 were $\exp(0.149) = 1.161$ times as likely to leave their workplaces as workers employed in 1987-1996. Therefore, if time consists of industrial deepening and partial relaxation of strict state labor controls in Korea, I suggest that industrial deepening and partial relaxation of strict state labor controls have increased employment stability in Korea.

Employment is generally more valuable and stable in heavy industry—where technologies and work organizations are more complex. The increase in the relative importance of heavy industry, therefore, has led to the increase in employment stability in Korea. In general, employment in more favorable structural positions in the labor market is more stable. Partial relaxation of strict state labor controls that began in 1987 has increased employment stability in Korea because they have enabled structural factors to play a more important role in determining wage levels.

The first implication of the nonsignificant estimated effects of the interactions of *ILM* with *Before 1961* and *1961 Through 1986* is related to the increase in the relative importance of heavy industry. The increase in the relative importance of heavy industry in the entire Korean economy over time has required higher levels of skills and knowledge of workers because heavy industry has more complex technologies and work organizations than light industry. The nonsignificant estimated effects of the above interactions imply that the degree of the increase in the relative importance of heavy industry in the entire Korean economy over time has not been so high as to cause significant maturation of job ladders that have existed in internal labor markets from the beginning. In other words, this implies that the degree of such increase has not been high enough to make job ladders in internal labor markets significantly longer and more complex.

The second implication of the nonsignificant estimated effects of the interactions of *ILM* with *Before 1961* and *1961 Through 1986* is related to partial relaxation of strict state labor controls since 1987. This relaxation of state labor controls has enabled job ladders to play a more important role in determining wage levels and working conditions. The nonsignificant estimated effects of the above interactions imply that the extent of this relaxation has not been so great as to cause significant maturation of job ladders that have existed in internal labor markets from the beginning.

One of the main reasons why industrial deepening and partial relaxation of state labor controls have not caused significant maturation of job ladders that have existed in internal labor markets from the beginning may be that the period of industrialization has been exceptionally short in Korea. In other words, there may not have been enough time for industrial deepening and partial relaxation of state labor controls to cause significant maturation of job ladders in the Korean internal labor market.

In sum, results about the estimated effects of an interaction between labor market structure and time show that the difference between the ability of internal labor markets to keep their workers and the ability of external labor markets to keep their workers has not changed significantly in Korea over time. I conclude that the difference between employment stability in internal labor markets and employment stability in external labor markets has not changed significantly in Korea over time.

Although there is no previous research on the effect of time on employment stability in other countries, the above results and discussion suggest the following arguments and prediction. In general, industrialization proceeds side by side with industrial deepening and relaxation of state labor controls, both of which constitute time in this study. Whether or not time affects employment stability in a country depends on the pace of industrial deepening and relaxation of state labor controls.

There are two reasons for this relationship. First, too slow a rate of increase in the relative importance of heavy industry means that the rate at which the overall complexity of technologies and work organizations in the entire economy increases is also too slow. This makes the overall increase in employment stability nonsignificant. Second, too slow a rate of relaxation of state labor controls means that the rate at which structural factors play a more important role in determining wage levels is also too slow. This makes the overall increase in employment stability nonsignificant. Therefore, if the pace of industrial deepening and relaxation of state labor controls is not too slow in a country, I expect that time increases employment stability in that country.

Cohort and Employment Duration

The estimated coefficients for *Cohort 1930s*, *Cohort 1940s*, and *Cohort 1950s*, which are included in the analysis to control for cohort size effects, are negative and significant. These results mean that in Korea over time, the cohort of workers born in the 1960s or later has been more likely to leave their workplace than each of the three cohorts of workers born in the 1950s or earlier.

The cohort of workers born in the 1960s or later is a larger cohort than each of the previous three cohorts of workers because (1) population growth has occurred, and (2) unlimited supply of unskilled labor from agricultural to industrial sectors had already ended when they entered the labor market (the Outline of the Study section of Chapter 1). Job matches for the cohort of workers born in the 1960s or later, therefore, have not been as good as job matches for the previous cohorts, which has led to a situation in which employment stability for the former is not as high as that for the latter.

The estimated coefficients for *Year 2* through *Year 10* and *Year 15* in Table 5-2 are positive and significant. These results show that in Korea, the probability of leaving a workplace significantly depends on the duration of working at the same workplace continuously. That is to say, in Korea, employment stability is lower in the early and late years of working at the same workplace than in the mid-years.

Conclusion

Results of the analysis in this chapter, by and large, simultaneously support theories on common factors of employment stability found in various countries and theories on factors of employment stability unique to Korea (represented by the variables for time)—if interactions between labor market structure and individual- and time-level factors are not considered.

Results of the analysis based on the binomial logit model including only main effects showed that all theoretical factors—labor market structure, human capital, gender and gender-related factors, organization-level characteristics, and time—have significantly affected employment stability in Korea. As suggested by the working hypotheses in Table 5-1, each of internal labor market structure, the highest amount compared to the lowest amount of general human capital, men, less childcare and housework responsibility, larger organizational size, unionism, and the later years compared to the earlier years of economic development has increased employment stability in Korea over time.

On the other hand, results of the analysis including interaction terms showed that labor market structure has barely affected differences in employment stability by individual- or time-level characteristics, whereas it has significantly affected differences in employment stability by organization-level characteristics in Korea over time. First, the estimated effects of interactions between labor market structure and each of human capital and gender and gender-related factors are not statistically significant. This means that in Korea over time, internal labor market structure has hardly increased differences in employment stability by individual-level characteristics.

Second, the estimated effects of an interaction between labor market structure and time are not statistically significant. This means that differences in employment stability between internal labor markets and external labor markets have remained unchanged over the course of Korea's economic development.

One of the most important factors contributing to these results may be that due to the exceptionally short period of Korea's industrialization, internal labor market structure in Korea has not been mature, i.e., complex and long, enough to influence the way in which individual- and time-level factors affect employment stability, although it has been mature enough to affect employment stability by itself.

Third, the estimated effect of an interaction between labor market structure and organizational size and the estimated effect of an interaction between labor market structure and unionism are statistically significant and in opposite direction to each other. This means that in Korea, internal labor market structure has increased differences in employment stability between large organizations and small organizations (as suggested by the relevant working hypothesis in Table 5-1), but decreased differences in employment stability between unionized organizations and nonunionized organizations. The latter result can be explained by a special characteristic of the Korean industrialization, that is, the stronger efforts of labor unions in external labor markets to overcome strict labor controls by the Korean state.

Results of the analysis based on the main-effects binomial logit model in this study can be compared with results from previous research. First, the effects of labor market structure, human capital, organizational size, and unionism on employment stability in Korea are consistent with results from previous research investigating the influences of the same factors in some Western countries, especially the United States. I argue that three conditions contribute to these consistencies: (1) A moderate degree of industrialization contributes to effects of labor market structure and organizational size, (2) an effective formal education system contributes to an effect of human capital, and (3) fairly active labor movements contribute to an effect of unionism. Furthermore, I predict that if these contributing factors also exist in a developing country, then labor market structure, human capital, organizational size, and unionism also significantly affect employment stability in that developing country.

Second, results of this study regarding the effects of gender and gender-related factors on employment stability in Korea are consistent with results from previous research showing the effects of these factors in some developing and advanced industrial countries. The pervasive effects of gender and gender-related factors on employment stability in different cultural and economic contexts implies that patriarchal values are widespread across many countries, restricting employment stability for female workers via institutional and cultural practices disadvantageous to women.

There is no previous research to which the effect of time on employment stability in Korea can be compared. On the basis of results of this study, however, I suggest that the effect of time on employment stability in a country depends on the pace of industrial deepening and relaxation of state labor controls. I expect, therefore, that time increases employment stability in a country unless the pace of industrial deepening and relaxation of state labor controls is very slow in that country.

There is also no previous research to which the investigation based on the interaction binomial logit model in this study can be compared. On the basis of results of this project, however, I predict how labor market structure influences the ways in which other factors affect employment stability in other countries.

First, the relative immaturity of the Korean internal labor market, which may have been caused by the exceptionally short period of Korea's industrialization, may have led to the situation in which labor market structure has not been able to affect differences in employment stability by any individual- or time-level characteristic. If this is the case, then labor market structure increases differences in employment stability by individual- or time-level characteristics if a country has achieved at least a moderate degree of industrialization over a longer time period.

Second, the result that internal labor market structure has increased differences in employment stability between large organizations and small organizations in Korea implies that job ladders in internal labor markets have been complex and long enough to increase the effect of organizational size on employment stability. However, they have not been complex and long enough to increase the effects of individual- and time-level factors on employment stability in Korea. In other words, despite its exceptionally short time period, Korea's industrialization has still been able to bring about the degree of maturity in internal labor markets needed for the labor market structure to influence the effect of organizational size on employment stability. From this, I predict that internal labor market structure increases the effect of organizational size on employment stability in countries that have achieved at least a moderate degree of industrialization, regardless of the pace of such industrialization.

Third, the finding that internal labor market structure has decreased differ-ences in employment stability between unionized organizations and nonunion-ized organizations is explained by the stronger efforts of labor unions in external labor markets to overcome strict state labor controls. Generally speaking, strict state labor controls are likely to be considerably relaxed in countries in which the degree of industrialization is very high. Therefore, if a country has achieved a very high degree of industrialization, internal labor market structure increases differences in employment stability between unionized organizations and nonunionized organizations in that country.

6 Desirability of Transition Outcomes

As suggested in Chapter 1, the desirability of transition outcomes is the second aspect of employment transitions related to workers' economic and social well-being in Korea. This chapter presents detailed working hypotheses regarding factors affecting the desirability of transition outcomes in Korea, discussions on whether or not results of the analysis support the working hypotheses, comparisons between results of this study and results from previous research, and a discussion of the implications of these comparisons for factors affecting the desirability of transition outcomes in countries other than Korea.

Working Hypotheses

The working hypotheses for both the main-effects ordered logit model and the interaction ordered logit model are presented in Table 6-1. They are based on definitions of the independent variables in Table 4-1 and on the predicted effects of the independent variables on the desirability of transition outcomes shown in Table 4-3. The rightmost column in Table 6-1 shows (1) whether or not each working hypothesis is supported by the result of the analysis in Table 6-2, and (2) if it is supported, whether it is supported partially or strongly.

Desirability of employment transition destinations is defined in Chapter 3. Thus, for workers who have left their workplaces, entrepreneurship is the most desirable new employment status, followed by employment in internal labor markets, self-employment, employment in external labor markets, and nonemployment, in order. The definitions of these new employment statuses are presented in Table 4-2.

Results of Analysis

Results of the analysis of factors affecting the desirability of transition outcomes in Korea are shown in Table 6-2. These include results from both the main-effects ordered logit model and the interaction ordered logit model.

Table 6-1. Working Hypotheses: Ordered Logit Models

Independent Variable	Working Hypothesis	Support From Result
Individual Level		
Education	• Workers with higher level of completed education are more likely to have better transition outcomes than workers with lower level of completed education.	Partial
	• The above tendency is stronger in internal labor markets (ILMs) than in external labor markets (ELMs).	No
Gender and Gender-Related Factors	• Female workers with few childcare and housework responsibilities (i.e., female workers who are unmarried and childless or whose youngest children are over 6 years of age) are more likely to have better transition outcomes than female workers with greater childcare and housework responsibilities (i.e., female workers who are married and before their first childbirths or whose youngest children are under 7 years of age).	Strong
	• The above tendency is stronger in ILMs than in ELMs.	No
	• Male workers are more likely to have better transition outcomes than female workers with greater childcare and housework responsibilities.	Strong
	• The above tendency is stronger in ILMs than in ELMs.	Strong
Structure Level		
Labor Market Structure	• Workers in ILMs are more likely to have better transition outcomes than workers in ELMs.	Strong
Organizational Size	• Workers in private organizations hiring more than 499 employees or in public organizations are more likely to have better transition outcomes than workers in private organizations hiring less than 500 employees.	No
	• The above tendency is stronger in ILMs than in ELMs.	No
Unionism	• Workers in unionized organizations are more likely to have better transition outcomes than workers in non-unionized organizations.	No
	• The above tendency is stronger in ILMs than in ELMs.	No

Table 6-1. Working Hypotheses: Ordered Logit Models (*Continued*)

Independent Variable	Working Hypothesis	Support From Result
Time	• Workers were less likely to have better transition outcomes before 1961 than in 1987-1996.	No
	• The degree to which workers in ILMs were more likely to have better transition outcomes than workers in ELMs was lower before 1961 than in 1987-1996.	No
	• Workers were less likely to have better transition outcomes in 1961-1986 than in 1987-1996.	No
	• The degree to which workers in ILMs were more likely to have better transition outcomes than workers in ELMs was lower in 1961-1986 than in 1987-1996.	No

A likelihood ratio test comparing fitted values from the main-effects model and the interaction model produces a chi-square statistic of 40.53 with 9 degrees of freedom and a significance level less than 0.00005. This result means that the interaction terms are jointly highly significant, and that the interaction model significantly improves the fit of the main-effects model.

Comparisons between signs of the coefficients in Table 6-2 and signs of the predicted effects of the independent variables on the probability of having more desirable transition outcomes shown in Table 4-3 are presented in Table 6-3.

Labor Market Structure

The estimated coefficient for *ILM* shows that for any fixed transition outcome except entrepreneurship, the estimated odds that a worker in an internal labor market has a more desirable transition outcome rather than a less desirable transition outcome equal exp(0.754) = 2.125 times the estimated odds for workers in an external labor market. The underlying mechanism for this result is that promotions on job ladders in the Korean internal labor market enable promoted workers to accumulate more material, intangible, or social assets that lead them to more desirable destinations than the structure of external labor markets.

There is no previous research on the effect of labor market structure on the desirability of transition outcomes, so that we cannot confirm empirically whether or not labor market structure also increases the desirability of transition outcomes in other developing countries and in industrially advanced countries.

Table 6-2. Results: Ordered Logit Models

Independent Variable	Main-Effects Model		Interaction Model	
	Coeffi-cient	Robust S.E.	Coeffi-cient	Robust S.E.
Individual Level				
Education (Reference: Elementary School or No Education)				
Middle School	0.409	0.311	0.397	0.344
High School	0.496	0.306	0.470	0.342
College	0.979**	0.318	0.877*	0.359
Gender and Gender-Related Factors (Reference: Female With Young Children)				
Female Without Young Children	1.526***	0.187	1.463***	0.205
Male	3.226***	0.187	2.905***	0.203
Structure Level				
ILM (Internal Labor Market)	0.754***	0.116	0.253	0.849
Large Organization	0.006	0.137	0.122	0.163
Unionized Organization	0.052	0.126	0.100	0.148
Time (Reference: 1987 Through 1996)				
Before 1961	0.094	0.664	0.193	0.745
1961 Through 1986	0.030	0.116	0.038	0.122
Interaction Terms				
Middle School×ILM			-0.100	0.827
High School×ILM			0.017	0.795
College×ILM			0.198	0.809
Female Without Young Children×ILM			-0.140	0.416
Male×ILM			1.046**	0.368
Large Organization×ILM			-0.449	0.291
Unionized Organization×ILM			-0.261	0.276
Before 1961×ILM			-0.184	1.325
1961 Through 1986×ILM			-0.020	0.230

Table 6-2. Results: Ordered Logit Models (*Continued*)

Independent Variable		Main-Effects Model		Interaction Model	
		Coeffi-cient	Robust S.E.	Coeffi-cient	Robust S.E.
Cohort (Reference: Born in 1961 or Later)					
	Cohort 1930s	-0.301	0.269	-0.308	0.273
	Cohort 1940s	-0.034	0.180	-0.020	0.182
	Cohort 1950s	0.123	0.129	0.148	0.126
Work Years		-0.031**	0.012	-0.031*	0.012
Cut Points					
	Cut Point 1	2.325	0.349	2.110	0.387
	Cut Point 2	3.959	0.359	3.765	0.394
	Cut Point 3	5.040	0.367	4.884	0.399
	Cut Point 4	7.228	0.389	7.128	0.419
Log-Likelihood		-2,644.559		-2,624.297	
Degrees of Freedom		2,264		2,255	
Number of Observations		2,282		2,282	

* $p < .05$, ** $p < .01$, *** $p < .001$ (two-tailed tests).

We expect, however, that internal labor market structure increases the desirability of transition outcomes in countries that have already achieved at least a moderate degree of industrial development. This is because the emergence of an internal labor market, which has a job ladder with entry port only at the bottom or with movement up this ladder, is closely related to a country's achievement of a moderate degree of industrial development.

Human Capital

The estimated coefficient for *College* shows that for any fixed transition outcome except entrepreneurship, the estimated odds that a worker with more than high school education has a more desirable transition outcome rather than a less desirable transition outcome equal $\exp(0.979) = 2.662$ times the estimated odds for workers with less than middle school education.

The other estimated coefficients for the variables of completed education are not statistically significant. I suggest, therefore, that the hypothesis about the

Table 6-3. Comparisons Between Predicted and Estimated Effects of
Independent Variables on Desirability of Transition Outcomes:
Ordered Logit Models

Independent Variable	Predicted Effect From Hypothesis	Estimated Effect From Analysis
Individual Level		
Education (Reference: Elementary School or No Education)		
Middle School	+	
High School	+	
College	+	+
Gender and Gender-Related Factors (Reference: Female With Young Children)		
Female Without Young Children	+	+
Male	+	+
Structure Level		
ILM (Internal Labor Market)	+	+
Large Organization	+	
Unionized Organization	+	
Time (Reference: 1987 Through 1996)		
Before 1961	−	
1961 Through 1986	−	
Interaction Terms (In Interaction Models)		
Middle School×ILM	+	
High School×ILM	+	
College×ILM	+	
Female Without Young Children×ILM	+	
Male×ILM	+	+
Large Organization×ILM	+	
Unionized Organization×ILM	+	
Before 1961×ILM	−	
1961 Through 1986×ILM	−	

effect of general human capital on the desirability of transition outcomes is
supported when the difference in the amount of general human capital is the
largest. This implies that in Korea, the amount of material, intangible, or social

assets, which are needed for workers to have better transition outcomes, is so large that only the largest difference in the amount of general human capital makes a significant difference in the probability of workers having better transition outcomes.

In Korea, the skill level of jobs for workers with the highest level of education is higher than that for workers with the lowest level of education. The expected gains from a job match rise with increases in the skill level of a job. Therefore, workers with the highest level of education have more chances of accumulating material assets at their current workplaces that help them have better transition outcomes than workers with the lowest level of education. Furthermore, the fact that compared to the latter, the former have higher levels of skills and knowledge and make more social relations during the time they receive more education means that they have more intangible and social assets helpful in moving on to better work positions elsewhere.

The mechanism for the nonsignificant estimated effects of the interactions between *ILM* and the variables for completed education is as follows. The degree to which workers with more general human capital accumulate more material, intangible, or social assets valuable to moving to better workplaces than workers with less general human capital is as high in internal labor markets as in external labor markets in Korea. This is because the degree to which job ladders in the Korean internal labor market (the higher positions of which are filled with workers having more general human capital) provide more material, intangible, or social assets for workers having more general human capital than for workers having less general human capital is as high as the degree to which the structure of the Korean external labor market does the same.

The result of the study mentioned in Chapter 3 that more general human capital is associated with more desirable transition outcomes in the United States (Tuma 1985) is consistent with the finding that more general human capital partially increases the desirability of transition outcomes in Korea. This may be because the effective formal education system makes it possible for higher formal education to produce actually more general human capital both in Korea and in an advanced industrial country such as the United States.

On the basis of this argument, I suggest that the effect of general human capital on the desirability of transition outcomes in developing countries other than Korea also depends on the effectiveness of the formal education system of those countries. In other words, I expect that more general human capital increases the desirability of transition outcomes in developing countries other than Korea if higher formal education produces more general human capital in those countries as well.

Gender

The estimated coefficient for *Female Without Young Children* shows that for any fixed transition outcome except entrepreneurship, the estimated odds that a female worker with few childcare and housework responsibilities has a more desirable transition outcome rather than a less desirable transition outcome equal $\exp(1.526) = 4.600$ times the estimated odds for female workers with greater childcare and housework responsibilities.

The estimated coefficient for *Male* shows that for any fixed transition outcome except entrepreneurship, the estimated odds that a male worker has a more desirable transition outcome rather than a less desirable transition outcome equal $\exp(3.226) = 25.179$ times the estimated odds for female workers with greater childcare and housework responsibilities.

Employers believe that female workers with few childcare and housework responsibilities and male workers are more productive and contribute more to increased profits than female workers with greater childcare and housework responsibilities. Therefore, they pay the former higher wages and assign them jobs requiring a higher degree of skill and knowledge. Institutional and customary practices based on patriarchal values allow the former to make social relations inside and outside the current workplace more easily. As a result, the former accumulate more material, intangible, or social assets at the current workplace that are helpful in having more desirable transition outcomes.

I suggested in the Operationalizing Independent Variables section of Chapter 4 that for employers, (1) female workers with greater childcare and housework responsibilities are the least desirable, (2) male workers are the most desirable, and (3) female workers with few childcare and housework responsibilities are in between. If this suggestion is correct, the absolute value of the coefficient for *Male* should be significantly greater than that for the coefficient for *Female Without Young Children*. This is confirmed by a statistical test: The chi-square statistic with 1 degree of freedom for the null hypothesis that the coefficient for *Female Without Young Children* is the same as the coefficient for *Male* is 213.55. The significance level for the test is less than 0.00005. Therefore, I reject the null hypothesis with great confidence and conclude that *Male* has a greater influence on the log odds of having more desirable transition outcomes than *Female Without Young Children*.

The mechanism for the significant estimated effect of the interaction between *Male* and *ILM* is as follows. Employers believe that male workers contribute more to the efficient operation of job ladders than female workers with greater childcare and housework responsibilities. As a result, job ladders in internal labor markets provide more promotion opportunities for the former than for the latter. Therefore, they provide more material, intangible, or social assets helpful in having better transition outcomes for the former than for the latter. Consequently, the tendency that male workers are more likely to have better transition outcomes than female workers with greater childcare and housework responsibilities is stronger in internal labor markets than in external labor markets in Korea.

The mechanism causing the nonsignificant estimated effect of the interaction between *Female Without Young Children* and *ILM* follows. Employers believe that female workers with few childcare and housework responsibilities contribute more to the efficient operation of job ladders than female workers with greater childcare and housework responsibilities. However, job ladders in the Korean internal labor market are not long and complex enough to provide the former with significantly more promotion opportunities. Therefore, they do not provide the former with significantly more material, intangible, or social assets helpful in having better transition outcomes. Consequently, the tendency that female workers with few childcare and housework responsibilities are more likely to have better transition outcomes is not stronger in internal labor markets than in external labor markets in Korea.

The finding that men and less responsibilities of childcare and housework increase the desirability of transition outcomes in Korea is consistent with results of studies mentioned in Chapter 3 showing the influences of marriage, childbirth, childcare, and household responsibilities on the desirability of transition outcomes for women in advanced industrial countries such as the United States and Japan, as well as in several developing countries including Korea. From this similarity, I infer that institutional and cultural practices based on patriarchal values, which cause less desirable transition outcomes for female workers, persist across many countries although their strength may vary.

Organization-Level Characteristics

The underlying mechanism for the nonsignificant estimated coefficient for *Large Organization* is that in Korea, (1) higher wages based on greater market power of large organizations, and (2) more chances of making social relations in large organizations are not enough to allow workers in large organizations to accumulate more material and social assets that help them move to better workplaces.

The mechanism for the nonsignificant estimated coefficient for *Unionized Organization* is that in Korea, the union wage effect based on workers' greater bargaining power in unionized organizations is not enough to allow workers in unionized organizations to save more earnings that help them move to better workplaces.

The nonsignificant estimated effect of an interaction between organizational size and labor market structure suggests that internal labor market structure does not change the fact that greater market power of large organizations and more chances of making social relations in large organizations do not increase the probability of having more desirable transition outcomes in Korea. Organizations with job ladders do not have significantly greater market power since relatively simple and short job ladders in the Korean internal labor market do not make the efficiency of work organizations significantly greater. In organizations with job ladders, workers do not have significantly more chances of making social relations with other higher-ranking workers who have more material or social resources since job ladders in the Korean internal labor market are relatively simple and short. Internal labor market structure, therefore, does not change the nonsignificant influence of organizational size on the desirability of transition outcomes in Korea.

The nonsignificant estimated effect of an interaction between unionism and labor market structure suggests that internal labor market structure does not change the fact that the union wage effect does not increase the probability of having more desirable transition outcomes in Korea. Relatively short and simple job ladders in the Korean internal labor market do not make higher positions on job ladders require workers to have significantly higher levels of skills and knowledge. Workers in internal labor markets, therefore, are not significantly more valuable to employers than workers in external labor markets. Workers in internal labor markets, therefore, do not have significantly greater bargaining power with employers than workers in external labor markets. As a result, internal labor market structure does not increase the union wages effect, not changing the nonsignificant influence of unionism on the desirability of transition outcomes in Korea.

The lack of previous research on the effect of organizational size on the desirability of transition outcomes does not allow empirical confirmation that organizational size does not affect the desirability of transition outcomes in other country contexts. However, considering the fact that organizational size does not affect the desirability of transition outcomes in Korea, a developing country, I suggest the following. A very high degree of industrialization, which makes market shares for large organizations exceptionally high and chances of making social relations for workers in large organizations very abundant, is needed for organizational size to affect the desirability of transition outcomes. Therefore, I expect that larger organizational size increases the desirability of transition outcomes only in highly advanced industrial countries.

The fact that unionism does not affect the desirability of transition outcomes in Korea is consistent with the fact that union membership affects neither the upward mobility of occupational prestige nor the upward wage mobility for inter-firm moves in the United States (Gu 1998). This consistency implies that the union wage effect based on labor unions' bargaining power is not strong enough to enable workers in unionized organizations to save more earnings helpful in moving on to better workplaces in both Korea and the United States.

One of the most important reasons for this implication may be that union density—the proportion of employed workers who are union members—has been relatively low in both countries. Union density was 15.8 percent in 1975, 14.7 percent in 1980, 12.4 percent in 1985, and 17.2 percent in 1990 in Korea (Tables

2-2 and 2-4), and 23.1 percent in 1975, 20.2 percent in 1980, 17.2 percent in 1985, and 18.0 percent in 1990 in the United States (Golden et al. 1999: 200). If union density is low in a country, the social pressure put on employers that employees who have been union members in their previous workplaces should not be at a disadvantage in terms of hiring, wages, and working conditions in their new workplaces is also likely to be low. In this situation, employers who can provide employees with higher wages and better working conditions may be reluctant to hire workers who have been union members in their previous workplaces because employers generally try to avoid unionization of their organizations or strengthening of existing unions. As a result, the union wage effect that allows workers in unionized organizations to save more earnings helpful in moving on to better workplaces may be offset to a significant degree.

On the basis of the above argument, I suggest that the effect of unionism on the desirability of transition outcomes in countries other than Korea and the United States depends on union density in those countries. More specifically, if union density is fairly high in a country, I expect that unionism increases the desirability of transition outcomes in that country. This phenomenon might be observed in some Western and Northern European countries where union density has traditionally been high (Golden et al. 1999: 198-202).

Time

If time reflects industrial deepening and partial relaxation of strict state labor controls in Korea, the nonsignificant estimated coefficients for *Before 1961* and *1961 Through 1986* suggest that industrial deepening and partial relaxation of strict state labor controls have not increased the desirability of transition outcomes in Korea. In general, workers save more earnings helpful in moving on to better workplaces in heavy industry in which technologies and work organizations are more complex. The period of increase in the relative importance of heavy industry, however, was not long enough to cause the increase in the desirability of transition outcomes in Korea. Workers in more favorable structural positions in the labor market generally save more earnings helpful in moving on to better work positions elsewhere. However, the period of relaxation of state labor controls that began in 1987 was not long enough to cause the increase in the desirability of transition outcomes in Korea: The period of such relaxation was not long enough to enable structural factors to play a more important role in determining wage levels.

Two mechanisms contribute to the nonsignificant estimated effects of the interactions of *ILM* with *Before 1961* and *1961 Through 1986*. First, the degree to which the increase in the relative importance of heavy industry required higher levels of skills and knowledge of workers was not so high as to facilitate significant maturation of the job ladder, i.e., the lengthening and complication of the job ladder. Second, the degree to which relaxation of state labor control policies since 1987 enabled the job ladder to play a more important role in determining wage levels was not so high as to facilitate significant maturation of the job ladder. As a result, the ability of internal labor markets to allow workers to accumulate material, intangible, or social assets that help them move to better workplaces did not become significantly greater than the ability of external labor markets to do the same in Korea.

On the basis of the above discussion, I predict the effect of time on the desirability of transition outcomes in other countries. Whether or not time affects the desirability of transition outcomes in a country depends on the duration of industrial deepening and relaxation of state labor controls in that country. There are two reasons for this. First, a brief period of increase in the relative importance of heavy industry means that the period needed for increase in the overall complexity of technologies and work organizations is also brief. This makes the overall increase in the desirability of transition outcomes nonsignificant. Second, a brief period of relaxation of state labor controls means that the period needed for structural factors to play a more important role in determining wage levels is also brief. This makes the overall increase in the desirability of transition outcomes nonsignificant. Therefore, if the period of industrial deepening and relaxation of state labor controls is not brief in a country, I expect that time increases the desirability of transition outcomes in that country.

Cohort and Employment Duration

The estimated coefficients in Table 6-2 for *Cohort 1930s, Cohort 1940s,* and *Cohort 1950s* are not statistically significant. These results mean that the cohort of workers born in the 1950s or before and the cohort of workers born in the 1960s or later show the same likelihood of having more desirable transition outcomes in Korea. It was pointed out in the *Cohort and Employment Duration* subsection of Chapter 5 that the larger size of the cohort of workers born in the 1960s or later and the discontinuance of unlimited supply of unskilled labor from agricultural to industrial sectors led the cohort of workers born in the 1960s or later to a situation in which job matches for them were not as good as job matches for the cohort of workers born in the 1950s. The same factors, however, did not lead to a situation in which the likelihood of having more desirable transition outcomes was lower for the former than for the latter.

The estimated coefficient in Table 6-2 for *Work Years* is negative and significant. This finding shows that for any fixed transition outcome except entrepreneurship, the estimated odds that a worker has a more desirable transition outcome rather than a less desirable transition outcome equal $\exp(-0.031) = 0.969$ times the estimated odds for workers who have stayed at the current workplace one year less. This result suggests that in Korea, the probability of having better transition outcomes significantly depends on the duration of working at the same workplace continuously. In other words, it shows that the longer workers stay at their current workplaces, the lower the likelihood of their having better transition outcomes in Korea.

Conclusion

Results of the analysis in this chapter support theories about the effects of common factors found in various countries, except organization-level factors and interactions between labor market structure and factors other than gender, on the desirability of transition outcomes. On the other hand, they do not support theories about the effects of factors unique to Korea, which are represented by the variables for time, on the desirability of transition outcomes in Korea.

Results of the analysis based on the ordered logit model including only main effects showed that only labor market structure and individual-level factors have significantly affected the desirability of transition outcomes in Korea over time as suggested by the working hypotheses in Table 6-1: Internal labor market structure, the highest amount compared to the lowest amount of general human capital, men, and less childcare and housework responsibility have increased the desirability of transition outcomes in Korea over time.

Meanwhile, results of the analysis including interaction terms showed that only the estimated effect of an interaction between labor market structure and gender is statistically significant as predicted. This means that in Korea over time, internal labor market structure has increased differences in employment stability between male workers and female workers with greater childcare and housework responsibilities, but has not increased differences in the desirability of transition outcomes by any other factor. Therefore, I suggest that overall, internal labor market structure has barely increased differences in the desirability of transition outcomes among Korean workers by increasing the desirability of transition outcomes for workers who have already had greater resources and been in various kinds of more favorable positions in the Korean labor market.

The fact that labor market structure has barely changed the effects of other factors on the desirability of transition outcomes implies the following. The degree of job ladder maturity, i.e., the complexity and length of job ladders in the Korean internal labor market, has not been so high as to intensify the advantages for workers who have already had greater resources and been in various kinds of more favorable positions in the Korean labor market in terms of desirability of transition outcomes. A special characteristic of Korea's industrialization, among others, may be responsible for the relatively low degree of job ladder maturity in the Korean internal labor market: The period of industrialization may have been too short for job ladders in the Korean internal labor market to become complex and long enough.

Results of the analysis based on the main-effects ordered logit model in this study can be compared with results from previous research. First, results of this study about the effects of human capital and unionism on employment stability in Korea are consistent with results from previous research investigating the effects of these factors on the desirability of transition outcomes in the United States. I argue that two conditions contribute to these consistencies: (1) An effective formal education system contributes to an effect of human capital, and (2) low union density contributes to a nonsignificant effect of unionism. From this argument, I expect that if a developing country has an effective formal education system and fairly high union density, the desirability of transition outcomes in that developing country is increased by more human capital and unionism, respectively.

Second, results of this study regarding the effects of gender and gender-related factors on the desirability of transition outcomes in Korea are consistent with results from previous research showing the effects of these factors on the desirability of transition outcomes in some developing and advanced industrial countries. The fact that gender and gender-related factors affect the desirability of transition outcomes in different cultural and economic contexts implies that patriarchal values, which decrease the desirability of transition outcomes for female workers via institutional and cultural practices disadvantageous to women, are widespread across many countries.

There is no previous research to which the effects of labor market structure, organizational size, and time on the desirability of transition outcomes in Korea can be compared. On the basis of results of this study, however, I suggest the following. (1) The effect of labor market structure depends on whether a country has already achieved at least a moderate degree of industrialization. (2) The effect of organizational size depends on whether the degree of industrialization is great. (3) The effect of time depends on the duration of industrial deepening and relaxation of state labor controls.

These suggestions lead to three expectations. (1) If a country has achieved at least a moderate degree of industrialization, internal labor market structure increases the desirability of transition outcomes in that country. (2) If a country has achieved a high degree of industrialization, larger organizational size increases the desirability of transition outcomes in that country. (3) If the period of industrial deepening and relaxation of state labor controls is not brief in a country, time increases the desirability of transition outcomes in that country.

There is also no previous research to which the interaction ordered logit model in this study can be compared. On the basis of results of this project, however, I predict how labor market structure influences the ways in which other factors affect the desirability of transition outcomes in other countries.

First, I suggest that the relative immaturity of the Korean internal labor market, which may have been caused by the exceptionally short period of industrialization, may have led to a labor market structure which has not affected differences in the desirability of transition outcomes by any factor considered in this study except gender. Thus, I expect that labor market structure increases differences in the desirability of transition outcomes by characteristics other than gender if a country has achieved at least a moderate degree of industrialization gradually over time.

Second, the result that internal labor market structure has increased differences in the desirability of transition outcomes between male workers and female workers with greater childcare and housework responsibilities has the following implications. Job ladders in internal labor markets have been complex and long enough to increase the effect of gender on the desirability of transition outcomes, although they have not been complex and long enough to increase the effect of other factors on the desirability of transition outcomes in Korea. In other words, although it has proceeded exceptionally rapidly, Korea's industrialization has still been able to establish internal labor markets mature enough to increase the effect of gender on the desirability of transition outcomes. I predict, therefore, that internal labor market structure increases the effect of gender on the desirability of transition outcomes in a country that has achieved at least a moderate degree of industrialization, whether it has achieved such industrialization rapidly or not.

7 Conclusion

The goal of this project was to investigate the effects of various theoretical factors, including labor market structure, on two aspects of employment transitions—employment stability and the desirability of transition outcomes—in Korea over time. In order to achieve this goal, theoretical models were developed based on previous theories and research that had mainly been developed and conducted in Western countries. Two kinds of statistical models—binomial logit models and ordered logit models—were specified that can best deal with event history data on employment stability and data on the desirability of transition outcomes, respectively. This final chapter presents a summary of results of the analysis, the implications of the results for two sociological questions posed in Chapter 1, the limitations of the study, and a future research agenda.

Summary

Theories that were developed in this study addressed both factors unique to Korea, which were represented by the variables for time, and other factors found in various countries. Results of the analysis, on the whole, supported theories about the effects of these two kinds of factors on employment stability more strongly than they supported theories about these effects on the desirability of transition outcomes.

Labor Market Structure

The most important task of this project was to investigate the effects of the structure of the Korean labor market on employment transition patterns. Furthermore, this project also tried to show whether or not the structure of the Korean internal labor market intensifies the effects of other factors on employment transition patterns.

Results of the analysis showed that overall, internal labor market structure has significantly increased employment stability and the desirability of transition outcomes in Korea over time. Internal labor market structure, however, was shown to have had no significant influences on the ways in which factors other than organizational size and unionism affect employment stability, and factors other than gender affect the desirability of transition outcomes. I suggest that this is due to the rapid industrialization of Korea, so that there has not been enough time for internal labor market structure to mature fully.

The only effect that was opposite to that predicted by the working hypothesis was the effect of an interaction between labor market structure and unionism on employment stability. This may be due to the stronger efforts of labor unions in external labor markets to overcome strict labor controls by the Korean state.

Other Factors

The effects of factors other than labor market structure on employment transition patterns in Korea were also investigated in this study. Results of the analysis showed that (1) while all other factors—human capital, gender and gender-related factors, organization-level characteristics, and time—have significantly affected employment stability as predicted by the working hypotheses, (2) only individual-level factors—human capital and gender and gender-related factors—have significantly affected the desirability of transition outcomes.

I explained the nonsignificant effects of organizational size, unionism, and time on the desirability of transition outcomes in Korea. First, insufficient advantages for large organizations over small organizations in terms of the complexity of technologies and market power are responsible for the nonsignificant effect of organizational size. Second, the weak union wage effect due to insufficient advantages for workers in unionized organizations over workers in nonunionized organizations in terms of bargaining power is responsible for the nonsignificant effect of unionism. Third, the period of industrial deepening and relaxation of strict state labor controls was not long enough to cause an effect of time.

Comparisons with Previous Research and Implications

Overall, there is not much research on the effects of factors considered in this study on employment transition patterns. Results of existing research, however, tend to be consistent with results of this study. I argued that some conditions common to both Korea and other researched countries are responsible for these similarities. (1) A moderate degree of industrialization leads to effects of labor market structure and organizational size on employment stability. (2) An effective formal education system leads to effects of human capital on employment stability and the desirability of transition outcomes. (3) Institutional and cultural practices based on patriarchal values lead to effects of gender and gender-related factors on employment stability and the desirability of transition outcomes. (4) Fairly active labor movements lead to an effect of unionism on employment stability. (5) Low union density leads to a nonsignificant effect of unionism on the desirability of transition outcomes.

The above conditions common to both Korea and other researched countries can be used to predict whether or not factors considered in this study also affect employment transition patterns in other countries, especially other developing countries. In other words, I expect that if these common conditions also exist in other developing countries, factors considered in this study affect employment transition patterns in those countries in the same way as in Korea and other researched countries.

If there is no previous research to which the effects of factors considered in this study can be compared, the discussion on results of this study can help predict the effects of those factors in other developing countries. I expect that if the conditions causing the effects of factors considered in this study also exist in other developing countries, those factors affect employment transition patterns in those countries in the same way as in Korea.

Implications of Results for Sociological Questions

On the basis of results of this study, I answer two sociological questions raised in Chapter 1: (1) How is the value that employers and workers place on stable employment modified by individual and structural factors? (2) How is the value that workers place on more desirable transition outcomes modified by individual and structural factors?

First, on the basis of results of the analysis on employment stability, I suggest that all factors considered in this study—internal labor market structure, more human capital, men, less childcare and housework responsibility, larger organizational size, unionism, and time—have significantly increased the value that employers and workers place on stable employment in Korea over time. Second, results of the analysis on the desirability of transition outcomes allow us to maintain that internal labor market structure and individual-level factors—more human capital, men, and less childcare and housework responsibility—have significantly increased the value that workers place on more desirable transition outcomes in Korea over time.

What do these answers mean to Korean workers' economic and social well-being over time? One needs to keep in mind that the overall level of Korean workers' economic well-being has increased due to Korea's rapid industrialization. For example, real wages have increased and working hours have decreased for Korean workers as shown in Chapter 2. The above answers address workers' subjective satisfaction with their material conditions, which is an important aspect of workers' social well-being. The fact that time has significantly increased the value that employers and workers place on stable employment implies that Korean workers' overall satisfaction with their material conditions has increased, too. This is consistent with the fact that the overall level of Korean workers' economic well-being has increased.

However, it also needs to be pointed out that several factors have increased differences in economic and social well-being among different types of workers in Korea. The internal labor market structure, more human capital, being male, having less responsibility for childcare and housework, larger organizational size, and unionism have more or less widened gaps in the level of economic and social well-being among Korean workers. Workers in external labor markets, workers with less human capital, female workers, workers with greater childcare and housework responsibilities, workers in small organizations, and workers in nonunionized organizations have also enjoyed the increase in economic and social well-being since the beginning of Korea's industrialization. However, socio-economic well-being has been significantly lower for them than for their respective counterparts, i.e., workers in internal labor markets, workers with more human capital, male workers, workers with less childcare and housework responsibilities, workers in large organizations, and workers in unionized organizations.

In sum, Korea's industrialization has had mixed effects on workers' economic and social well-being. On the one hand, it has improved the overall level of workers' well-being; on the other hand, it has increased heterogeneity in well-being among different types of workers. From the Korean experience, other industrializing countries can observe the mixed effects of industrialization on workers' economic and social well-being. Whether a developing country chooses to give priority to the overall increase in workers' well-being, or to improvement in the equity of well-being among different types of workers depends on how collective decision-making processes about this issue are restricted by the country's particular social, political, and historical context and international relations.

The fact that Korea's industrialization has had mixed effects on workers' economic and social well-being is significantly related to the consistent and considerable proportion of the self-employment sector as shown in Figure 1-4, which is an unusual characteristic of Korea's industrialization.[1] The considerable self-employment sector has played a role in convincing workers in unfavorable positions in labor markets, especially workers in external labor markets, to leave their current workplaces and seek new jobs in the self-employment sector. This has had mixed effects on workers' economic and social well-being.

First, by convincing workers in external labor markets to leave their current workplaces, the self-employment sector has decreased overall employment stability, and consequently, overall economic and social well-being of Korean workers. It is true that transitions of workers in external labor markets to self-employment can be considered upward mobility because workers in external labor markets tend to believe that self-employment increases their chances of greater economic success. However, as the finding that workers in internal labor markets have had more desirable transition outcomes than workers in external labor markets suggests, the gains that workers in external labor markets have had by moving to self-employment have been outweighed by the gains that workers in internal labor markets have had after leaving their current workplaces. This may have contributed to an increase in differences in economic and social well-being among different types of Korean workers.

Second, the considerable self-employment sector has played a role as a kind of social safety net by absorbing the social shock caused by unemployment, especially unemployment in external labor markets. Employment stability for workers in external labor markets is lower than that for workers in internal labor markets even if the self-employment sector does not convince workers in external labor markets to leave their current workplaces. In this situation, the existence of a considerable self-employment sector helps unemployed workers find new jobs in the self-employment sector easily, so that it lowers social tensions that a higher rate of unemployment might cause. This is especially true when an economy is in a recession that shrinks job opportunities in the employment sector.

The existence of a considerable self-employment sector in Korea reflects that the Korean employment sector has not provided an economically active population with enough job opportunities even though it has grown exceptionally fast. One important factor may be that the state's principal development strategy has been heavy-industrialization since the 1970s as shown in Chapter 2. Heavy industry is capital- and technology-intensive, so that it has lesser ability to provide job opportunities than light industry. Although it has increased Korea's national wealth rapidly, rapid heavy-industrialization has contributed to the existence of a considerable self-employment sector in Korea. We might say that in the long run, this situation does not facilitate an increase in the equity of economic and social well-being among Korean workers. The existence of a considerable self-employment sector may allow employers in the employment sector to take advantage of lower production costs in the self-employment sector through methods such as subcontracting. As a result, this will probably hinder good job opportunities in the employment sector, especially those in internal labor markets.

Whether a developing country chooses to give priority to a rapid increase in national wealth by initiating heavy-industrialization in its relatively early stage of development, or to improvement in the equity of workers' well-being in the longer term also depends on how collective decision-making processes about this issue are constrained by the country's particular social, political, and historical context and international relations.

This study dealt with Korea's industrialization through 1996. Korea encountered a major foreign exchange crisis in November 1997, which was a great blow to economic growth and workers' welfare. For example, the real GDP growth rate plunged from 5.0 percent in 1997 to -6.7 percent in 1998, and the unemployment rate soared from 2.6 percent in 1997 to 6.8 percent in 1998.[2] As a way of coping with the crisis, the state and capital opted for the strategy of labor market flexibilization by easing both the firing of employees and hiring various forms of part-time employees (Bai, 1999: 584-5). As a result, the ratio of part-time employees to full-time employees increased from 0.85 in 1997 to 1.10 in 2000.[3] This means that the overall level of Korean workers' economic and social welfare has considerably decreased in recent years. In this situation, the self-employment sector functioned as a social safety net to some degree— implied by the fact that the number of employees decreased by 0.64 percent from 1997 to 2000, while the number of the self-employed who did not hire any employees increased by 3.84 percent.[4] As mentioned above, however, this increase in the importance of the self-employment sector may decrease the equity of workers' welfare in the long run, since it may allow employers not to increase stable jobs in the employment sector.

As implied by the fact that the real GDP growth rate rebounded and reached 10.7 percent in 1999, the Korean economy can still be regarded as having the potential for continuing growth. However, the recovery of the Korean economy has been at the cost of workers' economic and social well-being. The deterioration of workers' welfare can be countered mainly by efforts on the part of workers themselves. In this regard, labor movements in Korea have shown conflicting signs in recent years. On the one hand, a considerable number of labor unions have conceded to employers' demands for lower wages, more flexible employment, and tougher working conditions in collective bargaining under the threat of mass dismissal (Bai, 1999: 590-1). On the other hand, the efforts of labor unions to overcome new challenges by the state and capital have intensified. Union density, which had continuously been falling from the peak of 18.7 percent in 1989 to the bottom of 11.2 percent in 1997, rose to 11.8 percent in 1999 and to 11.6 percent in 2000.[5] The number of union members, which had continuously been falling from the peak of 1.93 million in 1989 to the bottom of 1.40 million in 1998, rose to 1.48 million in 1999 and to 1.53 million in 2000.[6] The influence of more militant sects within labor movements has grown. The ratio of the number of union members belonging to the Korean Confederation of Trade Unions, which has been more militant against the state and capital, to the number of union members belonging to the Federation of Korean Trade Unions rose from 0.25 in 1995 to 0.41 in 2000.[7] Moreover, there have been signs of more cooperation between the two organizations in political and economic campaigns against the state and capital in recent years.

These efforts of Korean labor movements, however, face serious challenges from globalization as well as from the Korean state and capital. The collective bargaining structure in Western countries has been decentralized since the early 1980s (Katz, 1993). The decentralized bargaining structure in Western countries has been significantly influencing labor movements and labor markets in Third Word countries through the globalized economy and labor markets (Park, 2002:

63). Whether or not Korean workers' economic and social well-being will worsen in the near future will significantly depend on how effectively labor movements in Korea will respond to the strategy of labor market flexibilization by the state and capital and to the challenges from globalization, along with how effectively the state and capital will pursue this strategy and how the Korean economy will be affected by trends in the international political economy.

Limitations of the Study

Although they were the best available data, the original data used in this study had some limitations that hindered more thorough study of the subject. Most of all, due to the fact that the data were based on the retrospective interviews of individuals, the time unit could not be less than a year. This limitation led to the situation in which work spells whose durations were less than a year were presumably omitted from the data. Therefore, long-term patterns of employment stability and the desirability of transition outcomes in Korea may have been captured in this study less than perfectly. Furthermore, some of the independent variables were not truly time-varying, so that the influences of those independent variables on the instantaneous rates of employment transitions were analyzed imperfectly.

A limitation at a theoretical level can also be pointed out. Unlike theories on factors affecting employment stability, theories on factors affecting the desirability of transition outcomes were relatively weakly supported in this study. This means that there may be some other theoretical factors not specified in this study which affect the desirability of transition outcomes.

Future Research Agenda

The summary of results of this study, the summary of comparisons with previous research and their implications in other countries, and the discussion on the limitations of this study help propose a future research agenda. First of all, theories on factors affecting the desirability of transition outcomes need to be further developed in future research by specifying other relevant theoretical factors which affect the desirability of transition outcomes. It is also important to set up data in which these theoretical factors are represented by relevant variables.

Secondly, it is desirable to get data in which the time unit is precise enough and the independent variables are truly time-varying. If this kind of data is set up in the future, the effects of labor market structure and other relevant factors on employment transition patterns in Korea can be studied more accurately.

Thirdly, a comparative study on Korea and other countries, especially other developing countries, will help advance theories on employment stability and the desirability of transition outcomes presented in this study. If another developing country, in which the pattern and pace of industrialization have been different from those of Korea, is a subject of a comparative study, the conditions causing the effects of theoretical factors considered in this study can be further refined.

Notes

1 It is shown that the proportion of the self-employment sector has been significantly larger in Korea than in other developing countries similar in the degree of economic development to Korea (Kim 1987: 1-2; Choi 1999: 10-2).

2 The real GDP growth rates and the unemployment rates in this section are presented by the National Statistical Office.

3 The ratios are calculated based on the statistics presented by the National Statistical Office.

4 The percents are calculated based on the statistics presented by the National Statistical Office.

5 All union densities but that in 1989 are calculated based on the statistics presented by the National Statistical Office.

6 The statistics are presented by the Ministry of Labor.

7 The ratios are presented by the Ministry of Labor.

Appendix A

Relevant Questions From East Asia Social Survey

a1: In what year were you born?   19_____

a2: How old are you?

a3a1: Did you have any education after the age of 12?   1. Yes 2. No
a3a21-a3a28: How old were you when you entered and finished a school after the age of 12? (formal education)

a4a1: Have you ever been married? (including de facto- or re-marriage)
1. Yes 2. No
a4a21-a4a28: How old were you when you began and ended your marriage?
a4b1: Have you ever been separated or divorced?   1. Yes 2. No
a4b21-a4b28: How old were you when you became separated or divorced and ended being divorced or separated?
a4c1: Have you ever been widowed?   1. Yes 2. No
a4c21-a4c28: How old were you when you became widowed and ended being widowed?

a5a1: Do you have children?   1. Yes 2. No
a5a201-a5a212: How old were you when you had your child? (Please answer regarding all your children.)

Note (a6a1, a6b1, a601-a615): Now I would like to ask questions about your job experience. Here, a "job" means work you have done for at least one month after first leaving school, including working in your own business, in a family member's business, or doing piecework at home. It does not include part-time work during the school year, volunteer work, or hobby activities. If you held more than one job at a time, please answer about the main one. "Changing a job" means changing to another company or workplace. It does not include a promotion within the same company. For example, a person is regarded as having changed a job if s/he is currently a manager at company B whereas s/he was previously a manager at company A. But if a person got a promotion within the same company, it is not regarded as a change of job.

a6a1: Have you had a job since age 12?   1. Yes 2. No
a6b1: Have you ever changed jobs? 1. Yes 2. No
   a601-a615: How old were you when you began and ended a job?

a7k: (For male only) Have you completed military service?   1. Yes 2. No
   a7: From and to what age were you in military service?

b1: Gender   1. Male 2. Female

b3v: What is the highest level of education you have attained? (graduation or equivalence)
   1. No formal schooling
   2. Elementary school
   3. Middle school
   4. High school
   5. General high school
   6. Vocational high school
   7. Two-year college
   8. University
   9. Graduate study
   10. Other (specify: _____)

Note: I will now ask questions about your work experience (including your current work).

c41-c49: *(Interviewer: Referring to Part A (Calendar), enter according to the order of the job.)*

c4k1-c4k9: Between what ages did you have this job? *(Interviewer: Please check Part A (Calendar) to fill c4k1-c4k9. Please check with the respondent.)*

c91-c99: What is/was the total number of employees in the place you work/ed?
   1. 1 2. 2-4 3. 5-9 4. 10-29 5. 30-99 6. 100-499 7. 500 or more (or government institution)

c101-c109: In each job, including the current one, how many hours do/did you work per week?

c111: In the current job, what is your average annual income (including bonus, allowances, and taxes)?   0,000 won   *(Interviewer: If the respondent hesitates to answer, refer to* [card 3] *(c11av1).)*

      [card 3]   0. Refused to answer

               1. Below 3,000,000 won

               2. 3,000,000 – less than 9,000,000 won

               3. 9,000,000 – less than 15,000,000 won

               4. 15,000,000 – less than 21,000,000 won

               5. 21,000,000 – less than 30,000,000 won

               6. 30,000,000 – less than 40,000,000 won

               7. 40,000,000 – less than 50,000,000 won

               8. More than 50,000,000 won

c121-c129: What kind of work do/did you do? *(Interviewer: Ask only if the respondent is/was   not self-employed. If the respondent is currently self-employed, ask about previous jobs.)*

   1. Self-employed with employees

   2. Self-employed without employees

   3. Nonprofit organization employee

   4. Private company employee

   5. Government employee

   6. Nongovernment public sector employee

   7. Family enterprise worker without fixed pay

   8. Family enterprise worker with fixed pay

   9. Other (specify: _____)

c141-c149: By the time you left the job (or currently) are/were you in a managerial position?

   0. Not in a managerial position

   1. Lower-level manager

   2. Mid-level manager

   3. Top-level manager

c151-c159: By the time you left/leave this job, how did/would your company hire people with a similar rank to yours?

   1. Internally 2. Outside 3. Both internal promotion and hiring from outside

c161-c169: By the time you left/leave this job, did/would people of a similar rank to yours have a possibility of promotion?

   1. Not at all 2. Rarely 3. Sometimes 4. Frequently

c191-c199: Is/Was there a union where you work/worked?   1. Yes 2. No

(Interviewer: Check the respondent's current or most recent work experience (d6)).
    1. Has never had a job
    2. Worked/Working as an employee
    3. Self-employed, or working in a family business)

Note (d10, d11, d14): Only for those who answered 2 in d6, I would like to ask you some more questions about your current or most recent job.

d10: In this workplace, did you receive any formal training?   1. Yes 2. No

d11: Have you or any of your coworkers been transferred to a different position or place through a job rotation system in your company?   1. Yes 2. No

d14: How many times have you been promoted in this job?

If our society were divided into ten classes, in which class do you think your income and social status would belong? (1 means the lowest class; 10 means the highest class.)
    e151: Income _____ class
    e152: Social position _____ class

Appendix B

Weighting Variable for the Original Data (adapted from the document of the Korean part of East Asia Social Survey)

To facilitate comparison to the general population using the total sample of 3,570 persons, a weighting variable is provided. Applied to the total of both samples, this weighting variable approximates the distribution found in Census statistics. Specifically, the Census population is cross-tabulated by the following characteristics. In the data, the gender, age, occupation, and work form values are coded in the variable labeled "gajf" (gender, age, job, form) as follows.

	1	2	3	4	0
Gender	Male	Female			
Age	20-29	30-39	40-60		
Occupation	Clerical	Sales and Service	All Others		No Work
Form of Work	Owner/ Manager	Self-Employed	Employee	Family Worker	No Work

Each cell produced by cross-tabulating gender, age, occupation, and form of work was used in the following calculation of ratio weights:

Ratio Weight = (Proportion in Census) / (Proportion in Survey)

This ratio weight variable ranges in value from a low of 0.117 to a high of 5.0, with a mean of 0.9897.

Appendix C

Sampling Design

1. The nation is stratified into 22 life-zones based on major cities and their vicinities.
2. Each zone is classified into large cities, small- to medium-sized cities, and rural areas, so that 50 survey areas are formed.
3. Each survey area is clustered into strata by ward for large cities, by city for small- to medium-sized cities, and by county for rural areas.
4. Within each stratum of the survey area, in proportion to population size, 1 to 12 primary sampling units of wards, cities, or counties are selected using systematic random selection method.
5. Each primary sampling unit is clustered into strata by *dong* (village) for cities, by *eup* (rural community) or *myeon* (rural sub-community) for rural areas.
6. Within each stratum of the primary sampling unit, 1 to 5 secondary sampling units of *dongs*, *eups*, or *myeons* are selected using systematic random selection method.
7. In urban areas, the middle *tong* (sub-village) of a *dong* is selected as the tertiary sampling unit. In rural areas, after secondary sampling units are clustered by *ri* (the smallest rural community), one *ri* is selected as the tertiary sampling unit in each secondary sampling unit using systematic random selection method.
8. In urban areas, the middle *ban* (the lowest administrative unit) of a *tong* is selected as the fourth sampling unit. In rural areas, the middle *ban* of a *ri* or the central *burak* (small settlement within a *ri*) in relation to a *myeon* office is selected as the fourth sampling unit.
9. Every second household from the head of a *ban* or a *ri* in a certain direction is selected. Only one respondent is chosen from each household, and if the sex and age cohort of the respondent meet the predetermined criteria, that respondent is selected as the final respondent. The same procedures are repeated until the predetermined criteria about the proportions of sexes and age cohorts are reached. When selecting final respondents, the following are to be observed: (a) If there are two possible respondents with similar conditions in a household, the more economically active person is selected. (b) The distribu-

tions of the occupations of respondents are decided based on the distributions of the occupations in the same area. (c) In the fourth sampling unit, housewives cannot exceed half the married women. (d) There should be no more than one nonemployed person, excluding a housewife, or one student in the fourth sampling unit. (e) If the designated area is not a residential area, the supervising professor or researcher or his or her assistant can allow nearby *dongs* or *tongs* to be selected.

Bibliography

English Literature

Agresti, Alan. 1996. *An Introduction to Categorical Data Analysis*. New York, New York: John Wiley & Sons, Inc.

Allison, D. Paul. 1995. *Survival Analysis using the SAS® System: A Practical Guide*. Cary, North Carolina: SAS Institute Inc.

Althauser, Robert P. and Arne L. Kalleberg. 1981. "Firms, Occupations, and the Structure of Labor Markets: A Conceptual Analysis." In Ivar Berg, ed., *Sociological Perspectives on Labor Markets*. New York, New York: Academic Press, pp. 119-49.

Altonji, Joseph G. and Robert A. Shakotko. 1987. "Do Wages Rise with Job Seniority?" *Review of Economic Studies*, Vol. 54, No. LIV, pp. 437-59.

Amsden, Alice. 1992. *Asia's Next Giant: South Korea and Late Industrialization*. New York, New York: Oxford University Press.

Bai, Moo Ki and Woo Hyun Cho. 1995. *Women's Wages and Employment in Korea*. Seoul, Korea: Seoul National University Press.

Barreto, Humberto. 1989. *The Entrepreneur in Microeconomic Theory: Disappearance and Explanation*. New York, New York: Routledge.

Becker, Gary S. 1993. *Human Capital: A Theoretical and Empirical Analysis with Special Reference to Education*. Chicago, Illinois: The University of Chicago Press.

Blau, Francine D. and Lawrence M. Kahn. 1983. "Unionism, Seniority, and Turnover." *Industrial Relations*, Vol. 22, No. 3, pp. 362-73.

Blaug, Mark. 2000. "Entrepreneurship Before and After Schumpeter." In Richard Swedberg, ed., *Entrepreneurship: The Social Science View*. New York, New York: Oxford University Press, pp. 76-88.

Brinton, Mary C., Yean-Ju Lee, and William L. Parish. 1995. "Married Women's Employment in Rapidly Industrializing Societies: Examples from East Asia." *American Journal of Sociology*, Vol. 100, No. 5, pp. 1099-130.

Brouwer, Maria. 2000. "Entrepreneurship and Uncertainty: Innovation and Competition among the Many." *Small Business Economics*, Vol. 15, No. 2, pp. 149-60.

Carroll, Glenn R. and Karl Ulrich Mayer. 1986. "Job-Shift Patterns in the Federal Republic of Germany: The Effects of Social Class, Industrial Sector, and Organizational Size." *American Sociological Review*, Vol. 51, No. 3, pp. 323-41.

Casson, Mark. 1982. *The Entrepreneur: An Economic Theory*. Totowa, New Jersey: Barnes & Nobel Books.

Chin, Soo Hee. 1995. "The Determinants and Patterns of Married Women's Labor Force Participation in Korea." *Korean Journal of Population and Development*, Vol. 24, No. 1, pp. 95-129.

Dar, Amit. 1993. "The Dynamic Behavior of Job Mobility: A Specific Human Capital Approach." Ph.D. Dissertation, Brown University.

Deyo, Frederic C. 1989. *Beneath the Miracle: Labor Subordination in the New Asian Industrialism*. Berkeley and Los Angeles, California: University of California Press.

Doeringer, Peter B. and Michael J. Piore. 1985. *Internal Labor Markets and Manpower Analysis*. Armonk, New York: M. E. Sharpe, Inc.

England, Paula. 1992. *Comparable Worth: Theories and Evidence*. Hawthorne, New York: Aldine De Gruyter.

Felmlee, Diane H. 1980. "Women's Job Transitions: A Dynamic Analysis of Job Mobility and Job Leaving." Ph.D. Dissertation, University of Wisconsin-Madison.

————. 1982. "Women's Job Mobility Processes within and between Employers." *American Sociological Review*, Vol. 47, No. 1, pp. 142-51.

Freeman, Richard and James Medoff. 1984. *What Do Unions Do?* New York, New York: Basic Books.

Gereffi, Gary. 1990. "Paths of Industrialization: An Overview." In Gary Gereffi and Donald Wyman, eds., *Manufacturing Miracles: Paths of Industrialization in Latin America and East Asia*. Princeton, New Jersey: Princeton University Press, pp. 3-31.

Golden, Miriam A., Michael Wallerstein, and Peter Lange. 1999. "Postwar Trade-Union Organization and Industrial Relations in Twelve Countries." In Herbert Kitschelt, Peter Lange, Gary Marks, and John D. Stephens, eds., *Continuity and Change in Contemporary Capitalism*. New York, New York: Cambridge University Press, pp. 194-230.

Gu, Yanmin. 1998. "Labor Unions and Career Mobility of American Workers." Ph.D. Dissertation, Cornell University.

Katz, Harry C. 1993. "The Decentralization of Collective Bargaining: A Literature Review and Comparative Analysis." *Industrial and Labor Relations Review*, Vol. 47, No. 1, pp. 3-22.

Katz, Lawrence F. 1986. "Efficiency Wage Theories: A Partial Evaluation." In Stanley Fischer, ed., *NBER Macroeconomics Annual 1986*. Cambridge, Massachusetts: The MIT Press, pp. 235-76.

Kim, Byoung-Lo Philo. 1992. *Two Koreas in Development: A comparative Study of Principles and Strategies of Capitalist and Communist Third World Development.* New Brunswick, New Jersey: Transaction Publishers.

Kim, Eun Mee. 1997. *Big Business, Strong State: Collusion and Conflict in South Korean Development, 1960-1990.* Albany, New York: State University of New York Press.

Kim, Kyung-Ai. 1995. "Confucian Ideology on Women and Married Women's Participation in the South Korean Labour Force." In Barbara Einhorn and Eileen Janes Yeo, eds., *Women and Market Societies: Crisis and Opportunity.* Brookfield, Vermont: Edward Elgar Publishing Company, pp. 179-92.

Kirzner, Israel M. 1973. *Competition and Entrepreneurship.* Chicago, Illinois: The University of Chicago Press.

Koo, Hagen. 1990. "From Farm to Factory: Proletarianization in Korea." *American Sociological Review,* Vol. 55, No. 5., pp. 669-81.

Lang, Kevin and William T. Dickens. 1994. "Neoclassical and Sociological Perspectives on Segmented Labor Markets." In George Farkas and Paula England, eds., *Industries, Firms, and Jobs: Sociological and Economic Approaches.* Hawthorne, New York: Aldine de Gruyter, pp. 65-88.

Lee, Mijeong. 1998. *Women's Education, Work, and Marriage in Korea: Women's Lives Under Institutional Conflicts.* Seoul, Korea: Seoul National University Press.

Lewis, W. Arthur. 1954. "Economic Development with Unlimited Supplies of Labor." *Manchester School of Economic and Social Studies,* Vol. 22, pp. 139-91.

Marsden, Peter V. and Elizabeth H. Gorman. 2001. "Social Networks, Job Changes, and Recruitment." In Ivar Berg and Arne L. Kalleberg, eds., *Sourcebook of Labor Markets: Evolving Structures and Processes.* New York, New York: Kluwer Academic/Plenum Publishers, pp. 467-502.

Marsh, Robert M. and Hiroshi Mannari. 1971. "Lifetime Commitment in Japan: Roles, Norms, and Values." *American Journal of Sociology,* Vol. 76, No. 5, pp. 795-812.

Martinelli, Alberto. 1994. "Entrepreneurship and Management." In Neil J. Smelser and Richard Swedberg, eds., *The Handbook of Economic Sociology.* Princeton, New Jersey: Princeton University Press, pp. 476-503.

Mincer, Jacob. 1962. "On-the-Job Training: Costs, Returns, and Some Implications." *The Journal of Political Economy,* Vol. 70, pp. 50-79.

Mincer, Jacob and Boyan Jovanovic. 1981. "Labor Mobility and Wages." In Sherwin Rosen, ed., *Studies in Labor Markets.* Chicago, Illinois: The University of Chicago Press, pp. 21-63.

Oppenheimer, Valerie Kincade. 1982. *Work and the Family.* New York, New York: Academic Press.

Park, Young Jin. 1990. "Korean Patterns of Women's Labor Force Participation During the Period, 1960-1980." *Korean Journal of Population and Development*, Vol. 19, No. 1, pp. 71-90.

Petersen, Trond and Seymour Spilerman. 1990. "Job Quits from an Internal Labor Market." In Karl Ulrich Mayer and Nancy Brandon Tuma, eds., *Event History Analysis in Life Course Research*. Madison, Wisconsin: The University of Wisconsin Press, pp. 69-95.

Phang, Hanam. 1995. "A Dynamic Study of Young Women's Labor Market Transitions over the Early Life Course: Cohort Trends, Racial Differentials, and Determinants." Ph.D. Dissertation, University of Wisconsin-Madison.

Rebitzer, James B. 1986. "Establishment Size and Job Tenure." *Industrial Relations*, Vol. 25, No. 3, pp. 292-302.

Ripsas, Sven. 1998. "Towards an Interdisciplinary Theory of Entrepreneurship." *Small Business Economics*, Vol. 10, No. 2, pp. 103-15.

Ryan, Paul. 1981. "Segmentation, Duality and the Internal Labour Market." In Frank Wilkinson, ed., *The Dynamics of Labour Market Segmentation*. New York, New York: Academic Press, pp. 3-20.

Schumpeter, Joseph A. 1949. *The Theory of Economic Development: An Inquiry into Profits, Capital, Credit, Interest, and the Business Cycle*. Cambridge, Massachusetts: Harvard University Press.

————. 1976. *Capitalism, Socialism and Democracy*. New York, New York: Harper & Row, Publishers.

Sokoloff, Natalie J. 1980. *Between Money and Love: The Dialectics of Women's Home and Market Work*. New York, New York: Praeger.

Sørensen, Aage Bøttger. 2001. "Careers and Employment Relations." In Ivar Berg and Arne L. Kalleberg, eds., *Sourcebook of Labor Markets: Evolving Structures and Processes*. New York, New York: Kluwer Academic/Plenum Publishers, pp. 295-318.

Swedberg, Richard. 2000. "The Social Science View of Entrepreneurship: Introduction and Practical Applications." In Richard Swedberg, ed., *Entrepreneurship: The Social Science View*. New York, New York: Oxford University Press, pp. 7-44.

Tilly, Chris and Charles Tilly. 1994. "Capitalist Work and Labor Markets." In Neil J. Smelser and Richard Swedberg, eds., *The Handbook of Economic Sociology*. Princeton, New Jersey: Princeton University Press, pp. 283-312.

————. 1998. *Work under Capitalism*. Boulder, Colorado: Westview Press.

Topel, Robert. 1986. "Job Mobility, Search, and Earnings Growth: A Reinterpretation of Human Capital Earnings Functions." In Ronald G. Ehrenberg, ed., *Research in Labor Economics*. Greenwich, Connecticut: JAI Press Inc., pp. 199-233.

Tsuya, Noriko, Larry L. Bumpass, and Minja Kim Choe. 2000. "Gender, Employment, and Housework in Japan, South Korea, and the United States." *Review of Population and Social Policy*, Vol. 9, pp. 195-220.

Tuma, Nancy Brandon. 1972. "Stochastic Models of Social Mobility: A Comparative Analysis and an Application to Job Mobility of Mexican-American Men." Ph.D. Dissertation, Michigan State University.

————. 1985. "Effects of Labor Market Structure on Job Shift Patterns." In James J. Heckman and Burton Singer, eds., *Longitudinal Analysis of Labor Market Data*. New York, New York: Cambridge University Press, pp. 327-63.

Wade, Robert. 1990. "Industrial Policy in East Asia: Does It Lead or Follow the Market?" In Gary Gereffi and Donald Wyman, eds., *Manufacturing Miracles: Paths of Industrialization in Latin America and East Asia*. Princeton, New Jersey: Princeton University Press, pp. 231-66.

Walby, Sylvia. 1986. *Patriarchy at Work: Patriarchal and Capitalist Relations in Employment*. Minneapolis, Minnesota: University of Minnesota Press.

Wallace, Michael and Arne L. Kalleberg. 1981. "Economic Organization of Firms and Labor Market Consequences: Toward a Specification of Dual Economy Theory." In Ivar Berg, ed., *Sociological Perspectives on Labor Markets*. New York, New York: Academic Press, pp. 77-117.

Woo, Jung-eun. 1991. *Race to the Swift: State and Finance in Korean Industrialization*. New York, New York: Columbia University Press.

Yamaguchi, Kazuo. 1992. "Accelerated Failure-Time Regression Models with a Regression Model of Surviving Fraction: An Application to the Analysis of "Permanent Employment" in Japan." *Journal of the American Statistical Association*, Vol. 87, No. 418, pp. 284-92.

Yellen, Janet L. 1984. "Efficiency Wage Models of Unemployment." *The American Economic Review*. Vol. 74, No. 2, pp. 200-5.

Yoo, Tae-In Chung. 1996. "Korean Firms and Their Internal Labor Markets." Ph.D. Dissertation, State University of New York at Stony Brook.

Korean Literature

Bai Moo Ki. 1989. *Labor Economics [Nodong Gyeongjehak]*. Seoul, Korea: Gyeongmunsa.

————. 1991. *Labor Relations and Employment in Korea [Hangugui Nosa Gwangyewa Goyong]*. Seoul, Korea: Gyeongmunsa.

————. 1999. "Changes in Environments and Conditions of Labor Relations and Implications [Nosagwangye Hwangyeong, Jogeonui Byeonhwawa Geu Hamui]." In Cho Woo Hyun and Bai Moo Ki, eds., *Labor Economy in Korea: Issues and Prospects [Hangugui Nodong Gyeongje: Jaengjeomgwa Jeonmang]*. Seoul, Korea: Gyeongmunsa, pp. 577-602.

Cho Woo Hyun. 1992. *Theories on Reforms in Labor Relations* [*Nosa Gwangye Gaehyeongnon*]. Seoul, Korea: Changbi Publishers.

Choi Ho-Young. 1999. "A Study on the Self-Employed Workers in Korea [Hangugui Jayeongeop Bumune Gwanhan Yeongu]." Ph.D. Dissertation, Kookmin University.

Jung I-Hwan. 1992. "The Change of Internal Labor Market and Industrial Relations in Manufacturing Industry in Korea [Jejoeop Naebu Nodong Sijangui Byeonhwawa Nosa Gwangye]." Ph.D. Dissertation, Seoul National University.

Kim Dae-Hwan. 1991. "Social Role and Political Activities of Korean Labor Unions [Hanguk Nodongjohabui Sahoejeok Yeokhalgwa Jeongchihwaldong]." In Labor Education and Research Institute, ed., *Labor Problems in Korea* [*Hangugui Nodong Munje*]. Seoul, Korea: Bibong Publishers, pp. 197-219.

Kim Hyeongbae. 1982. "A Review of Labor Laws for the Last 35 Years [Nodong Beopje 35nyeonui Hoego]." In *Yearbook of Labor Economy* [*Nodong Gyeongje Yeongam*]. Seoul, Korea: Korea Employers Federation, pp. 189-209.

Kim Jae Ho. 1987. "A Study on Urban Petty Self-Employed in Korea [Hangugui Dosi Yeongse Jayeongeopjae Gwanhan Yeongu]." M.A. Thesis, Yonsei University.

Kim Kyung-Ai. 1999. *Labor and Sexuality of Korean Women* [*Hanguk Yeoseongui Nodonggwa Sexuality*]. Seoul, Korea: Pulbit Publishing.

Kim Taehong. 1996. *Reemployment Structure and Employment Policies for Women* [*Yeoseong Jaechwieop Gujowa Goyong Jeongchaek Gwaje*]. Seoul, Korea: Korean Women's Development Institute.

Kim Yeong-Ok. 1999. *A Dynamic Analysis of Women's Career Mobility* [*Yeoseong Chwieomnyeogui Dongtaejeogin Byeonhwa Bunseok*]. Seoul, Korea: Korean Women's Development Institute.

Kim Yonghak, An Gyechun, Song Ho-Keun, Yee Jaeyeol, and Kim Hyeokrae. 1999. "A Comparative Study of Labor Markets in Korea and Taiwan [Hangukgwa Daemanui Nodongsijang Bigyo Yeongu]." Unpublished Research Report. Seoul, Korea.

Korea Labor Institute (KLI). 1998. *KLIDB 2.0*. CD-ROM. Seoul, Korea: KLI.

Lee Joung Woo. 1991. "A Study of Korean Workers' Conditions [Hangugui Nodongjasangtae Daehan Ilgochal]." In Labor Education and Research Institute, ed., *Labor Problems in Korea* [*Hangugui Nodong Munje*]. Seoul, Korea: Bibong Publishers, pp. 297-321.

National Statistical Office (NSO). 1998. *Statistical Review on Socio-Economic Changes in the Republic of Korea for the Last 50 Years* [*Tonggyero Bon Daehanminguk 50nyeonui Gyeongje Sahoesang Byeonhwa*]. CD-ROM. Seoul, Korea: Inter VEG.

Park Joon-Shik. 2002. *Globalization and Labor Regime* [*Segyehwawa Nodong-cheje*]. Seoul, Korea: Hanul Academy.

Shin Kwang-Yeong. 1994. *Class and Politics of Production* [*Gyegeupgwa Nodong Undongui Sahoehak*]. Seoul, Korea: Nanam Publishing House.

Song Ho-Keun. 1991. *Labor Politics and Market in Korea* [*Hangugui Nodong Jeongchiwa Sijang*]. Seoul, Korea: Nanam Publishing House.

————. 1995. *Korea's Company Welfare: An Empirical Research* [*Hangugui Gieop Bokji Yeongu*]. Seoul, Korea: Korea Labor Institute.

Yee Jaeyeol. 1996. *Economic Sociology: Theory and Method of Micro-Macro Link* [*Gyeongjeui Sahoehak: Misi-Geosi Yeongye Bunseogui Irongwa Bangbeop*]. Seoul, Korea: Nanam Publishing House.

Yee Sangryun. 1983. "A Review of Labor Policies for the Last 35 Years [Nodong Jeongchaek 35nyeonui Hoego]." In *Yearbook of Labor Economy* [*Nodong Gyeongje Yeongam*]. Seoul, Korea: Korea Employers Federation, pp. 203-44.

Yu Yeong-hi. 1996. "An Event History Analysis of Women's Labor Market Transitions [Yeoseongui Nodongsijang Jeonhwane Gwanhan Sageonsa Bunseok]." M.A. Thesis, Hallym University.

Index

About the Author

Kim Sunghoon received his Ph.D. from Brown University in the United States in May, 2002. The title of his doctoral dissertation is "Effects of Labor Market Structure on Employment Stability and Desirability of Transition Outcomes in South Korea." He received his Master's degree from Hallym University in South Korea. He is currently full-time lecturer in the department of social studies education at Ewha Womans University, South Korea. His areas of interest are labor markets, social networks, development, and methodology.